Investigating Sophomore Student Success:

National Survey of Sophomore-Year Initiatives and the Sophomore Experiences Survey, 2014

Dallin George Young, Laurie A. Schreiner, and Eric J. McIntosh

Cite as:

Young, D. G., Schreiner, L. A., & McIntosh, E. J. (2015). *Investigating sophomore student success: The National Survey of Sophomore-Year Initiatives and the Sophomore Experiences Survey, 2014* (Research Reports No. 6). Columbia, SC: University of South Carolina, National Resource Center for The First-Year Experience & Students in Transition.

ISBN: 978-1-889271-95-8
Published by:
National Resource Center for The First-Year Experience® and Students in Transition
University of South Carolina
1728 College Street, Columbia, SC 29208
www.sc.edu/fye

Production Staff for the National Resource Center:

Project Manager:	Toni Vakos, Editor
Design and Production:	Joey Hilton, Graphic Artist
External Reviewers:	Ryan D. Padgett, Assistant Vice President for Student Success and Assessment, Northern Kentucky University.
	Molly Schaller, Assistant Professor and Coordinator of the College Student Personnel Program and a Fellow in the Learning Teaching Center, University of Dayton

---

Library of Congress Cataloging-in-Publication Data

Young, Dallin George.
 Investigating sophomore student success : the national survey of sophomore-year initiatives and the sophomore experiences survey, 2014 / Dallin George Young, Laurie A. Schreiner, & Eric J. McIntosh.
    pages cm. -- (Research reports on college transitions ; no. 6)
 Includes bibliographical references.
 ISBN 978-1-889271-95-8
 1. College sophomores--United States. 2. College students--United States. I. Schreiner, Laurie A. II. McIntosh, Eric J. III. Title.
 LA229.Y65 2015
 378.1'98--dc23
                    2015007235

About the Publisher

The National Resource Center for The First-Year Experience and Students in Transition was born out of the success of University of South Carolina's much-honored University 101 course and a series of annual conferences on the freshman-year experience. The momentum created by the educators attending these early conferences paved the way for the development of the National Resource Center, which was established at the University of South Carolina in 1986. As the National Resource Center broadened its focus to include other significant student transitions in higher education, it underwent several name changes, adopting the National Resource Center for The First-Year Experience and Students in Transition in 1998.

Today, the Center collaborates with its institutional partner, University 101 Programs, in pursuit of its mission to advance and support efforts to improve student learning and transitions into and through higher education. We achieve this mission by providing opportunities for the exchange of practical and scholarly information as well as the discussion of trends and issues in our field through the convening of conferences and other professional development events, such as institutes, workshops, and online learning opportunities; publishing scholarly practice books, research reports, a peer-reviewed journal, electronic newsletters, and guides; generating, supporting, and disseminating research and scholarship; hosting visiting scholars; and maintaining several online channels for resource sharing and communication, including a dynamic website, listservs, and social media outlets. The National Resource Center serves as the trusted expert, internationally recognized leader, and clearing house for scholarship, policy, and best practice for all postsecondary student transitions.

Institutional Home

The National Resource Center is located at the University of South Carolina's (UofSC) flagship campus in Columbia. Chartered in 1801, the University's mission is twofold: (a) to establish and maintain excellence in its student population, faculty, academic programs, living and learning environment, technological infrastructure, library resources, research and scholarship, public and private support, and endowment; and (b) to enhance the industrial, economic, and cultural potential of the state. The Columbia campus offers 324 degree programs through its 14 degree-granting colleges and schools. Students have been awarded more than $20 million for national scholarships and fellowships since 1994. In fiscal year 2014, faculty generated $230 million in funding for research, outreach, and training programs. UofSC is one of only 63 public universities listed by the Carnegie Foundation in the highest tier of research institutions in the United States.

Acknowledgements

The authors would like to acknowledge Sara Frakes for her analytical contributions to this research brief and the financial support of the Faculty Research Council at Azusa Pacific University for maintaining the Thriving InCollege website (www.thrivingincollege.org) and underwriting the survey costs.

Contents

List of Tables and Figures

Tables

Figures

Introduction

This report is a team effort by researchers at the National Resource Center for The First-Year Experience and Students in Transition and The Thriving Project at Azusa Pacific University (APU) to gather information at the student and institutional levels to better understand the second college year. The partnership was driven by a desire to increase our knowledge of sophomore student characteristics, institutional efforts to attend to this population, and students' perception about their learning and development. Findings from two parallel research projects are presented: (a) the National Survey of Sophomore-Year Initiatives (NSSYI), administered by the National Resource Center, with a focus on institution-level data, and (b) the Sophomore Experiences Survey (SES), conducted by The Thriving Project at APU, a student-level instrument. The NSSYI was previously administered in 2005 and 2008, and the SES has been continuously administered since 2007; however, in 2014, researchers at the two institutions coordinated the data collection of both instruments to yield a more complete picture of the sophomore year.

Why Continue to Study the Sophomore Year?

Although less is known about the sophomore year compared to other college transition points, such as the first and senior years, the past 20 years have seen increased attention in the literature and in campus programming to better understand and serve second-year students. The sophomore year can be a time of wonder and exploration, presenting opportunities "for turning inward and for exploring how one fits into college life and the world at large" (Schaller, 2010, p. 13). However, students in the second year have also been branded as forgotten, invisible, disillusioned, and dispiriting (Boyer Commission, 1998; Pattengale & Schreiner, 2000; Tobolowsky, 2008). Sophomores have been referred to as the academy's middle children (Gahagan & Hunter, 2006), and, for many students, the experience has long been characterized as a slump (Freedman, 1956), full of student inertia and confusion (Tobolowsky, 2008).

Several factors common in the sophomore year can trigger these paradoxical responses. Sophomores typically begin to wrestle with substantive questions that range from *why am I taking these classes* to *what is the purpose and meaning of my life* (Margolis, 1989; Schaller, 2005). Students shift from uncertainty and random exploration toward a focused approach aimed at attaining more than simple enjoyment from their educational experiences (Schaller, 2005). In addition, deciding on a major and a career path are important choices that second-year students make and may be the most salient issue they face (Coburn & Treeger, 1997; Gahagan & Hunter, 2006; Gardner, 2000). Yet, students must make the critical decision of settling on a specific educational track while simultaneously engaging in a broad array of general education and introductory courses—and often without the same level of faculty engagement, advisement, or support they experienced in their first year. Moreover, involvement is still being solidified as these students make choices about study abroad, service-learning, civic engagement, and other important engagement opportunities, again, often with limited support (Schreiner, Louis, & Nelson, 2012). Further, for traditional-age students, the second year represents an opportunity for significant personal development. It is a time when students begin to face the struggle between external and internal authority and expectations— reconciling newly learned beliefs with familial or past convictions and developing self-authorship (Baxter Magolda, King, Taylor, & Wakefield, 2012; Coburn & Treeger, 1997).

1

The sophomore-year experience can be quite different at four-year institutions compared to two-year schools. Second-year students at four-year colleges and universities are more likely to attend full time (U.S. Department of Education, 2013) and have aspirations for a bachelor's degree (Leigh & Gill, 2003). Their second year tends to be focused on developing a sense of self and making choices about majors and, ultimately, career paths. Sophomores at two-year institutions are less likely to attend full-time (U.S. Department of Education, 2013), yet they must still grapple with the same issues of purpose and direction—with more imminent implications. Decisions about next steps, such as transferring or entering the workforce, are at the forefront; however, the time frame is condensed, particularly for those who attend full-time. For the campus professionals who serve these students, the sophomore year at a two-year institution is, in effect, equivalent to the senior year at a four-year college in terms of the transition, career, academic, and support services that need to be provided. Moreover, with greater numbers of part-time and nontraditional students, defining the sophomore year (e.g., by credits earned, the number of semesters or years attending the college, and/or life or work experience) in two-year institutional contexts can be challenging (Jones & Franco, 2010).

Despite ongoing calls to create an integrated undergraduate experience across all years (Boyer Commission, 1998; Keeling, 2004; Kuh, 2010; Kuh, Kinzie, Schuh, & Whitt, 2005), the sophomore year has fewer high-impact programs and curricular offerings compared to other years, particularly in four-year institutions (Barefoot, Griffin, & Koch, 2012). A national survey conducted by Barefoot et al. (2012) found the college experience is front-loaded with summer bridge programs, orientation, first-year seminars, and multiple engagement opportunities, while on the back end (i.e., junior and senior years) lie internships, undergraduate research prospects, and senior capstone experiences. Even peer leadership positions may not be available to students at many four-year institutions until the third year (Graunke & Woosley, 2005; Tobolowsky, 2008). As a result, sophomores receive the least attention of any class, making fewer contacts with faculty and garnering less support from student affairs staff (Pattengale & Schreiner, 2000).

Finally, after first-year students, sophomores are the group at highest risk of attrition (Gardner, Pattengale, Tobolowsky, & Hunter, 2010; Lipka, 2006; Noel-Levitz, 2013). Moreover, Keup, Gahagan, and Goodwin (2010) found evidence that institutions with sophomore success initiatives have higher retention rates than those without them. As the number of institutions providing (or in the process of establishing) second-year programs continues to grow (Keup et al., 2010; Gardner et al., 2010; Tobolowsky & Cox, 2007), research is warranted to identify the types of initiatives that are being offered and determine the conditions under which students will flourish.

Theoretical Framework

Underlying the desire to combine our efforts in this research partnership was an assumption that institutional efforts influence student outcomes. This assumption was based on the Input-Environment-Outcome (I-E-O) theoretical framework first introduced by Astin (1991) and which serves as the basis for many student success models (Kennedy & Upcraft, 2010). In any educational situation, students come prepackaged with a variety of personal attributes (e.g., ability, motivation, experience, culture, achievement) representing *inputs*. The *environment* includes the curricular and cocurricular activities offered to students. These programs are developed to produce some kind of change, that is, to have an impact on *student* outcomes. This model provides educators a way to better isolate and evaluate the effectiveness of educational experiences on resulting student learning and development. As such, the I-E-O model served as our framework, with results presented and analyzed from this point of view.

Organization of This Report

Investigating Sophomore Student Success is divided into three sections: (a) an overview of the NSSYI, (b) an overview of the SES, and (c) an integrated discussion of the results from both research efforts and their implications for practice and ongoing research on sophomore student success. In addition, the appendices provide a list of the participating institutions; the survey questions; the frequency distributions of responses to the NSSYI questions, disaggregated by institutional characteristics (i.e., type, control, and size of undergraduate enrollment); and the national norms for the SES. The information and tables in this report will provide useful tools for institutions looking for benchmarks, to create new sophomore-year programs, or to restructure existing initiatives.

National Survey of Sophomore-Year Initiatives: Institutional Environments

The 2014 National Survey of Sophomore-Year Initiatives (NSSYI) was conducted to gather information about the current state of institutional efforts focused on second-year students in the United States. This was the third administration, following studies conducted in 2005 and 2008. The aim of the 2014 NSSYI was to collect evidence about institutional attention to the sophomore year; expand knowledge about specific institutional programs, services, and initiatives offered to this population; and investigate educationally effective practices present in second-year student success programs.

Survey Instrument

The 2014 questionnaire was created by the National Resource Center for The First-Year Experience and Students in Transition, based on modifications to the 2008 instrument. The number of sophomore initiatives was expanded from 20 to 33, and two new sections were added to the instrument, one asking about the overall institutional attention to the sophomore year and a second concerning elements of high-impact practices (HIPs). Survey dissemination and administration were conducted with web-based technology using the CampusLabs Baseline platform, a product of HigherOne, Incorporated.

Overall, the instrument was structured around the following sections: (a) institutional information, (b) institutional attention to the sophomore year, (c) current sophomore-year initiatives, (d) coordination of sophomore-year initiatives, (e) primary institutional initiative, (f) students, (g) characteristics of the initiative, (h) educationally effective practices, (i) administration of the primary initiative, and (j) assessment and evaluation. In addition, the questionnaire asked respondents who indicated that their institution did not offer sophomore-specific initiatives to report on any past or future sophomore initiatives. The full questionnaire is presented in Appendix A.

Survey Administration

The survey was targeted to individuals responsible for second-year programming, as identified by respondents from the 2012-2013 National Survey of First-Year Seminars (NSFYS); chief academic officers (CAOs); chief executive officers (CEOs); and/or chief student affairs officers (CSAOs) at regionally accredited, undergraduate-serving institutions of higher education, listed in the *Higher Education Directory*. The CAOs, CEOs, and/or CSAOs were invited to participate via e-mail and asked, if necessary, to forward the request to the most appropriate campus representative to ensure respondents were knowledgeable about the sophomore programming at each institution.

Administration of the survey began on March 18, 2014. The first wave of invitations was sent to individuals named as responsible for second-year programs on campus by NSFYS respondents. CAOs, CEOs, and CSAOs were then contacted in succession to provide responses on behalf of their institutions. If the CAO, CEO, or CSAO was not listed in the *Higher Education Directory* or the person responsible for second-year programs was not listed in the NSFYS, the institution was omitted from the study. Nonverified or undeliverable e-mail accounts were also omitted from the study.

The invitation served three main purposes: to (a) notify participants that the National Resource Center was conducting an administration of the survey; (b) provide detailed information about when they could anticipate receiving a link to the survey instrument; and (c) confirm that the participant was the appropriate contact and representative who could accurately provide information about second-year programming, and if not, request the correct campus contact information.

At survey launch, a total of 3,722 institutions were invited to participate. The institutions were e-mailed the survey link and given until May 31, 2014 to complete the form. Following each wave of invitations, follow-up reminders were sent to nonrespondents. A final reminder was e-mailed to all groups of institutional contacts. To give institutions ample time to respond to the final reminder, the survey remained open until June 6, 2014. A total of 778 unique colleges and universities responded to the NSSYI, an effective response rate of 20.9%. While this denotes a lower than expected rate for web-based surveys, typically around 25% (Gunn, 2002; Wang, Dziuban, & Moskal, 2000), it represents a sizeable increase in the total number of participating institutions, up from 382 in the 2005 administration and 315 in 2008. While the low response rate is a limitation, the sample in this study represents the most comprehensive picture of institutional practice related to sophomore students to date. Appendix B presents the list of participating institutions that have given permission to include their names.

Participating Institutions

Table 1 presents a comparison of the sample of campuses responding to the NSSYI to a national profile of institutions in the United States. The percentages in the table show that four-year institutions are slightly overrepresented in the sample of respondents. The sample also includes a smaller proportion of campuses with 1,000 or fewer undergraduate students than the national percentage. Finally, private, for-profit institutions were greatly underrepresented in the sample. Because of the small number of participating for-profit colleges and universities in the survey and recognizing these institutions operate in unique ways with respect to their students, they are not included in comparisons based on institutional control.

Table 1
Comparison of Institutional Characteristics

Institutional characteristic	National percentage (*N* = 4,516)	Percentages of all campuses responding to NSSYI (*N* = 778)
Type		
Two-year	35.3	22.9
Four-year	64.7	77.1
Control		
Public	36.9	54.1
Private, not-for-profit	37.3	42.9
Private, for-profit	25.8	3.0
Undergraduate enrollment		
Fewer than 500 students	24.6	6.2
501-1,000 students	14.3	7.4
1,001-1,500 students	9.3	8.6
1,501-3,000 students	17.7	25.0
3,001-5,000 students	10.1	12.6
5,001-10,000 students	11.8	17.3
10,001-15,000 students	5.2	8.9
15,001-20,000 students	2.9	6.1
More than 20,000 students	4.1	7.9

Note. Figures for the national percentages are from the Integrated Postsecondary Education Data System by the National Center for Education Statistics (2014).

Analyses

The analyses of the sample data were primarily conducted at the descriptive level. Comprehensive frequency distribution and sample percentages for each item reported throughout the research brief were tabulated in the aggregate (total) across institutional type, control, and size. Significant effects are reported throughout the research brief. The majority of items included were categorical variables, and significance was determined using the chi-square test for fit of distribution. To address adequate expected cell counts (i.e., least 20% of the cells with expected counts of five or more), analyses were not conducted when any actual cell counts were less than five. This is noted in all tables throughout the report where such analyses were not conducted.

The findings from the 2014 NSSYI have been organized in selected areas based on the following four research questions:

- To what extent and in what ways are colleges and universities attending to sophomore students at the institution level?
- What are the characteristics of initiatives, programs, and services aimed directly at sophomores?
- What are the sophomore-specific initiatives that reach the largest proportion of students on campuses and what are their characteristics?
- To what extent are elements of high-impact practices present in primary sophomore-year initiatives?

Results highlight the student learning environment and those structures that might have the most proximate impact on it. Although several questions from the instrument will not be discussed in this report, frequencies for all responses to the NSSYI are available in Appendix C.

Institutional Attention to Sophomores

The 2014 administration of the NSSYI introduced a series of questions about institutional attention to the sophomore year. This section addresses those questions covering institutional efforts focused on the sophomore year, the length of time second-year programs or initiatives have been in place, and the institutional objectives for this cohort.

Institutional Efforts Focused on the Sophomore Year

Respondents were asked to identify campuswide institutional efforts that included a specific focus on the sophomore year. As presented in Table 2, the most frequently reported institutional effort was to conduct a retention study (40.7%). In addition, approximately a quarter of institutions stated their institutional assessment (28.0%) and strategic planning (25.8%) undertakings targeted sophomores. Other campuswide activities were named, including creating a sophomore-experience task force, considering sophomores in the design of the general education curriculum, and offering campuswide professional development centered on those who work with second-year students. However, the largest group of respondents (41.6%) indicated their campuses were not engaged in any wide-scale attention to the sophomore year.

Table 2
Institutional Efforts Focused on the Sophomore Year

Institutional effort	Total	
	Freq.	%
Retention study	317	40.7
Institutional assessment	218	28.0
Strategic planning	201	25.8
Program self-study	123	15.8
National survey	114	14.7
Accreditation	81	10.4
Grant-funded project	71	9.1
Other	49	6.3
None of these	324	41.6
Total	778	100.0

When campuswide efforts are disaggregated by institutional type (Table 3), results show that two-year colleges more often include attention to sophomores in their accreditation processes ($p < .05$). Four-year institutions more frequently reported considering the second year as a point of emphasis in retention studies or participation in a national survey ($p < .05$). Table 4 presents a breakdown of institutional efforts by control and reveals no differences between private and public colleges and universities in the rates at which they report campuswide efforts including a focus on the second year.

Table 3
Efforts Focused on the Sophomore Year by Institutional Type ($n = 778$)

Institutional effort	Institutional type					
	Two-year		Four-year			
	Freq.	%	Freq.	%	Difference (%)	*p*
Percentages larger for two-year institutions						
None of these	85	47.8	239	39.8	8.0	*
Accreditation	28	15.7	53	8.8	6.9	
Grant-funded project	20	11.2	51	8.5	2.7	
Institutional assessment	53	29.8	165	27.5	2.3	
Program self-study	29	16.3	94	15.7	0.6	
Percentages larger for four-year institutions						
Retention study	60	33.7	257	42.8	-9.1	*
National survey	17	9.6	97	16.2	-6.6	*
Strategic planning	37	20.8	164	27.3	-6.5	
Other	10	5.6	39	6.5	-0.9	
Total	178	100.0	600	100.0	0.0	

*$p < .05$.

Table 4
Efforts Focused on the Sophomore Year by Institutional Type (n = 755)

	Institutional control				
	Public		Private		
Institutional effort	Freq.	%	Freq.	%	Difference (%)
Percentages larger for public institutions					
None of these	183	43.5	135	40.4	3.1
Grant-funded project	44	10.5	25	7.5	3.0
Other	28	6.7	20	6.0	0.7
Percentages larger for private institutions					
National survey	57	13.5	55	16.5	-3.0
Strategic planning	102	24.2	89	26.6	-2.4
Program self-study	64	15.2	54	16.2	-1.0
Accreditation	41	9.7	35	10.5	-0.8
Retention study	167	39.7	135	40.4	-0.7
Institutional assessment	118	28.0	95	28.4	-0.4
Total	421	100.0	334	100.0	0.0

Note. None of the comparisons in the table were statistically significant.

Length of Time Institutions Have Focused on the Sophomore Year

If respondents indicated they had included a specific focus on the sophomore year in their institutional efforts, they were asked to report how long they had been doing so. Figure 1 displays the amount of time institutions have been including a focus on sophomores in their campuswide efforts. Nearly 80% of institutions who reported incorporating second-year issues in these efforts have done so for five years or less. Conversely, there is a sizeable contingent (21.6%) of institutions who have had a focus on sophomores in their efforts for six years or more, including 8.5% with initiatives spanning more than a decade and 3.0% with programs in place for more than 20 years. A comparison by institutional type and control found no differences in the length of time respondents have paid particular attention to the sophomore year.

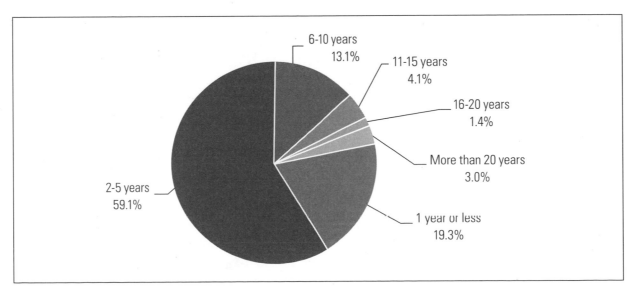

Figure 1. Length of time institutional efforts have focused on the sophomore year (*n* = 435).

Objectives for the Sophomore Year

Respondents who included sophomores in campuswide efforts were also asked to identify the objectives their institutions had created specifically for their students' second year. Overall, the five most frequently reported objectives were (a) retention (62.1%), (b) career exploration (53.5%), (c) career preparation (45.4%), (d) academic assistance (45.1%), and (e) selection of a major (44.9%). These objectives are consistent with the literature on the needs of second-year students and with the findings of the previous administrations of the NSSYI (Keup et al., 2010; Tobolowsky & Cox, 2007). Additionally, 11.6% of participants cited other objectives, with the most prevalent including preparation for study abroad, preparation for internships, successful transition from first to second year, successful transition from second to third year, moving from second year to completion, preparation to transfer to four-year institutions, academic skills, development of social networks, and professional licensing.

Table 5 shows the institutional objectives for the sophomore year disaggregated by institutional type. Two-year colleges were more likely to select graduation rates, career preparation, student satisfaction, critical-thinking skills, and oral communication skills ($p < .05$ or lower). The objectives identified by four-year institutions, at significantly higher levels ($p < .05$ or lower), included selection of a major, connection with the institution, self-exploration, and developing a support network or friendships. These patterns of objectives are consistent with the differing missions of two- and four-year colleges and universities. Two-year institutions are working to provide second-year students with the skills necessary to graduate and enter the next phase, whether gaining employment or transferring to continue their education. Four-year institutions have more time with sophomores to support their success, which includes helping students decide on a major and developing a sense of belonging on campus—necessary steps toward the completion of a bachelor's degree.

Table 5
Sophomore-Year Objectives by Institutional Type (n = 441)

| Institutional effort | Institutional type | | | | Difference (%) | p |
| | Two-year | | Four-year | | | |
	Freq.	%	Freq.	%		
Percentages larger for two-year institutions						
Graduation rates	57	61.3	81	23.3	38.0	***
Career preparation	57	61.3	143	41.1	20.2	***
Student satisfaction	40	43.0	91	26.1	16.9	**
Critical-thinking skills	30	32.3	73	21.0	11.3	*
Oral communication skills	24	25.8	57	16.4	9.4	*
Financial literacy	24	25.8	63	18.1	7.7	
Intercultural competence	17	18.3	49	14.1	4.2	
Student-faculty interaction	25	29.6	103	26.9	2.7	
Information literacy	15	16.1	47	13.5	2.6	
Other	12	12.9	39	11.2	1.7	
Civic responsibility	24	25.8	85	24.4	1.4	
Percentages larger for four-year institutions						
Selection of a major	20	21.5	178	51.1	-29.6	***
Connection with institution	13	14.0	139	39.9	-25.9	***
Self-exploration	10	10.8	107	30.7	-19.9	***
Support network or friendship	9	9.7	70	20.1	-10.4	*
Institutional resources	15	16.1	85	24.4	-8.3	
Career exploration	44	47.3	192	55.2	-7.9	
Preprofessional preparation	4	4.3	40	11.5	-7.2	a
Writing skills	16	17.2	77	22.1	-4.9	
No campuswide objectives specifically for sophomores	5	5.4	35	10.1	-4.7	
Leadership opportunities	37	39.8	155	44.5	-4.7	
Student engagement	37	39.8	153	44.0	-4.2	
Academic skills	27	29.0	113	32.5	-3.5	
Service-learning	25	26.9	103	29.6	-2.7	
Study skills	18	19.4	74	21.3	-1.9	
Academic assistance	41	44.1	158	45.4	-1.3	
Retention	57	61.3	217	62.4	-1.1	

Note. The sum of the percentages is larger than 100% due to the ability of respondents to select more than one response.
[a]Analysis was not conducted due to cell counts less than five.* $p < .05$. ** $p < .01$. *** $p < .001$.

Disaggregating the objectives by institutional control (Table 6) revealed that public colleges and universities in the sample more frequently ($p < .05$ or lower) identified graduation rates and financial literacy as important for sophomores. Private institutions reported self-exploration and connection with the institution at significantly higher rates ($p < .05$ or lower).

Table 6

Sophomore-Year Objectives by Institutional Control ($n = 425$)

	Institutional control					
	Public		Private			
Sophomore-year objective	Freq.	%	Freq.	%	Difference (%)	*p*
Percentage larger for public institutions						
Graduation rates	98	42.4	36	18.6	23.8	***
Retention	151	65.4	110	56.7	8.7	
Financial literacy	52	22.5	27	13.9	8.6	*
Critical-thinking skills	59	25.5	36	18.6	6.9	
Academic assistance	104	45.0	83	42.8	2.2	
Other	30	13.0	21	10.8	2.2	
Oral communication skills	42	18.2	31	16.0	2.2	
Study skills	48	20.8	36	18.6	2.2	
Career preparation	107	46.3	86	44.3	2.0	
Information literacy	32	13.9	23	11.9	2.0	
Student engagement	99	42.9	80	41.2	1.7	
Service-learning	69	29.9	55	28.4	1.5	
Civic responsibility	58	25.1	46	23.7	1.4	
Academic skills	72	31.2	59	30.4	0.8	
Writing skills	46	19.9	38	19.6	0.3	
Student satisfaction	66	28.6	55	28.4	0.2	
Percentage larger for private institutions						
Self-exploration	48	20.8	64	33.0	-12.2	**
Connection with institution	69	29.9	76	39.2	-9.3	*
Leadership opportunities	91	39.4	92	47.4	-8.0	
Support network or friendship	33	14.3	41	21.1	-6.8	
Career exploration	118	51.1	110	56.7	-5.6	
Intercultural competence	31	13.4	31	16.0	-2.6	
Student-faculty interaction	64	27.7	57	29.4	-1.7	
No campuswide objectives specifically for sophomores	20	8.7	20	10.3	-1.6	
Selection of a major	105	45.5	91	46.9	-1.4	
Preprofessional preparations	21	9.1	20	10.3	-1.2	
Institutional resources	51	22.1	43	22.2	-0.1	

Note. The sum of the percentages is larger than 100% due to the ability of respondents to select more than one response.

* $p < .05$. ** $p < .01$. *** $p < .001$.

Characteristics of Sophomore-Year Initiatives

Administrations of the NSSYI have attempted to provide the most up-to-date and comprehensive examination of adoption, type, features, and objectives of initiatives specifically designed to support students in the second college year. This section provides an overview of sophomore-year initiatives, focusing on their presence on campuses, their coordination, and the types being offered.

Presence of Sophomore-Year Initiatives

When asked about the presence of initiatives specifically or intentionally geared toward sophomore students, 46.1% ($n = 349$) of respondents indicated their institution offered one or more. Institutions with sophomore-specific programs are more likely to respond to a survey focused on such programs, which would inflate the estimate of the prevalence of such programs on campuses. However, this represents a considerable increase in the prevalence found in the 2005 and 2008 NYSSI administrations, 33.5% and 36.5% respectively (Keup et al., 2010; Tobolowsky & Cox, 2007), despite nearly doubling the number of institutions participating in the survey ($N = 778$ in 2014, $N = 382$ in 2005). This, along with the recent attention to sophomore-year issues reported (i.e., 80% of respondents indicated focusing on these issues for five years or less), provides further evidence that programs aimed at students in the second year of college continue to grow in prevalence.

When the sample of institutions in the current administration is disaggregated by type (Figure 2), significantly ($p < .01$) more four-year institutions (49.4%) reported offering sophomore-specific initiatives than two-year institutions (35.1%). Similarly, when the rates are broken down by institutional control (Figure 3), significantly ($p < .05$) more private institutions (50.3%) offer sophomore initiatives than do public colleges and universities (42.5%).

However, it is important to understand these differences in historical context. In the 2008 administration of the NSSYI, 28.4% of public institutions reported offering sophomore initiatives, a lower rate than privates (45.6%). Even more strikingly, only 11.7% of two-year institutions offered any sophomore-year initiatives compared to 44.5% of their four-year counterparts. Thus, the growth in the adoption of sophomore-year initiatives appears to be happening at greater rates at public institutions and, in particular, at two-year colleges.

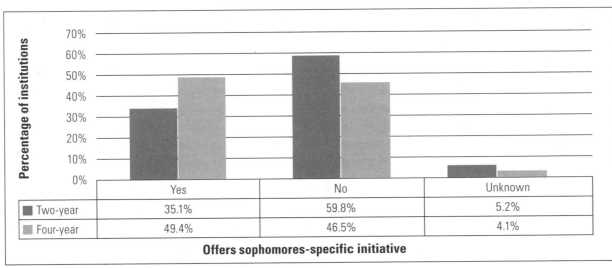

	Yes	No	Unknown
■ Two-year	35.1%	59.8%	5.2%
■ Four-year	49.4%	46.5%	4.1%

Offers sophomores-specific initiative

Figure 2. Institutions offering sophomore-specific initiatives by institutional type ($n = 757$). $p < .01$.

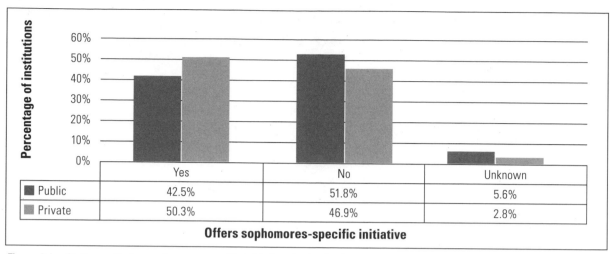

Figure 3. Institutions offering sophomore-specific initiatives by institutional control ($n = 735$). $p < .05$.

Centralization of Efforts

When asked to rate the degree of coordination of sophomore initiatives on a 5-point scale from 1 = *totally decentralized* to 5 = *totally centralized*, the largest group of institutions (35.5%) reported the coordination of their sophomore initiatives fell in the middle spot between complete coordination and autonomy. A slightly larger group of institutions indicated less centralization of initiatives (1 or 2 on the scale, 38.1%) than those with more centralization (3 or 4 on the scale, 25.6%). This suggests that, overall, sophomore-year initiatives fall somewhere between completely centralized and decentralized. However, the distribution leans slightly toward a less coordinated approach across institutions.

A breakdown of responses by institutional type reveals differences in the coordination of initiatives (Figure 4). Significantly ($p < .05$) more four-year institutions reported greater levels of coordination than two-year colleges. More than half of all two-year institutions stated the level of coordination of sophomore programs as decentralized (represented by values of 1 or 2 on the scale). Similar patterns were observed when disaggregating the responses by institutional control (Figure 5). Private colleges and universities had significantly ($p < .01$) greater levels of coordination than public ones. Approximately half of public campuses indicated that second-year programs and initiatives were not centralized (represented by values of 1 or 2 on the scale).

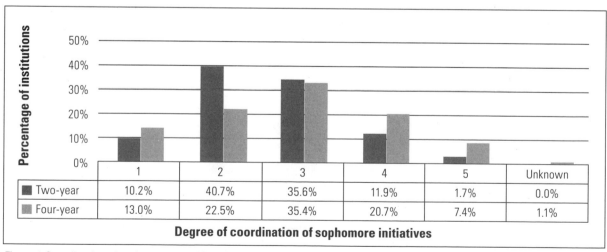

Figure 4. Coordination of sophomore-specific initiatives by institutional type. 1 = *Totally decentralized,* 5 = *Totally centralized.* $p < .05$.

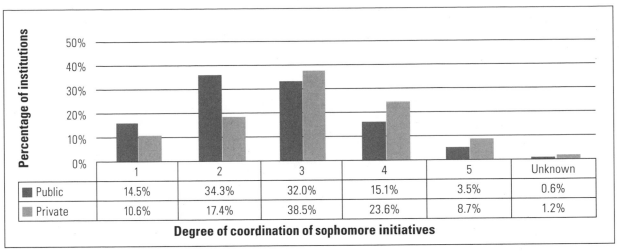

Figure 5. Coordination of sophomore-specific initiatives by institutional control. 1 = *Totally decentralized,*
5 = *Totally centralized. p < .01.*

Another marker of coordination is whether the institution has given the responsibility of sophomore student programs or initiatives to an individual on campus. Nearly one third (33.1%) of institutions with sophomore-year initiatives reported having an individual in charge. This proportion decreased greatly since the 2008 administration of the NSSYI where 58.3% of respondents identified an individual with this responsibility on campus (Keup et al., 2010). This marks a decrease in the proportion of institutions with a person responsible for sophomore programs in the face of the increased incidence of these initiatives. These patterns suggest that sophomore-year initiatives are expanding in specific functional areas across campus, such as career services, academic advising, and residential life, and, consequently, there are relatively fewer specifically designated individuals with responsibility for overseeing the array of second-year services.

As highlighted earlier in the report, the growth in these programs is occurring more frequently among two-year and public institutions. These two groups are less likely to be centralized, thus lending support to the idea of programs emerging in areas across campus first and then working toward collaboration and coordination later. However, without information about the age of the specific sophomore initiative as well as the motivating factors for centralization, including a person responsible for second-year programs, we cannot be sure this is the case. More research is warranted to understand the noticeable growth of these programs and how institutions are working to coordinate the numerous efforts designed to support sophomores.

Types of Sophomore-Year Initiatives

To gain an understanding of the ways in which institutions were supporting sophomore student success, the 2014 NSSYI asked responding campuses to identify the types of services, programs, and resources available. The questionnaire included a list of 33 success initiatives along with an *other* category, and institutions indicated which of these initiatives were currently offered for sophomore students (a full list of sophomore-year initiatives can be found in the questionnaire in Appendix C). These 33 initiatives were developed through previous iterations of the NSSYI, drawing primarily on open-ended responses to include new options that respondents could identify. Figure 6 presents the 10 most frequently reported sophomore-year initiatives.

Academic advising and career exploration were the most frequently reported initiatives; more than half of responding institutions sponsored these programs. The popularity of career-related support programs (career exploration and planning) is consistent with the findings from the 2008 NSSYI. Keup et al. (2010) found career planning was the most widely adopted sophomore-specific program, with 76.7% of respondents offering that initiative. The 2014 administration of the survey offered institutions the option of choosing either career exploration or career planning to describe their program, while in the 2008 NSSYI, respondents only had career planning as an option to capture career-related initiatives. When career exploration and planning were combined, 61.4 % of institutions reported offering career-related programs to sophomores, making it the most frequently identified initiative.

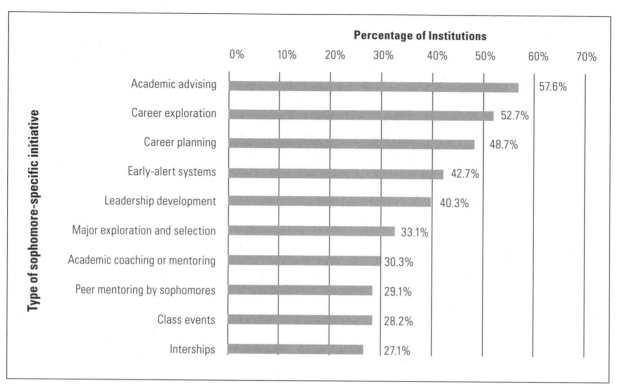

Figure 6. Types of sophomore-specific initiatives offered (*n* = 347). *Note.* The sum of the percentages is larger than 100% due to the ability of respondents to select more than one response.

The proportion of institutions offering sophomore-specific academic advising remained virtually unchanged since the 2008 NSSYI (57.7% in 2008, 57.6% in 2014). However, leadership development (58.8% in 2008, 40.3% in 2014) and class events (50.9% in 2008, 28.2% in 2014) both decreased in prevalence. Given the increased size of the sample of responding institutions and the lack of longitudinal data, interpretation of these changes is difficult. What is clear is that academic advising and career-related programs have been long-standing and widely adopted initiatives aimed at supporting success among sophomore students, a result consistent with the findings of Keup et al. (2010).

Another 10.4% of respondents reported *other* types of sophomore-year initiatives that were not included in the list of options presented, such as academic support programs (e.g., tutoring, writing, online resources), course-based initiatives, career co-op programs, sophomore-specific curricula, awards and scholarships, social events (e.g., faculty and alumni dinner), and auto-credentialing for students who had met criteria for degree completion.

Disaggregating the variety of sophomore-year initiatives by institutional type (Table 7) revealed some noteworthy patterns and differences. Two-year colleges were two-to-three times more likely to offer programs centered on internships ($p < .001$) and financial aid ($p < .001$) as well as summer bridge programs ($p < .05$). Four-year campuses offered services to sophomores focused on major exploration and selection at ($p < .001$) at twice the rate of two-year institutions. Despite these differences, academic advising and career-related initiatives remain among the most frequently identified initiatives at both two- and four-year institutions.

Table 7
Sophomore-Specific Initiatives by Institutional Type (n = 347)

	Institutional type					
	Two-year		Four-year			
Institutional effort	Freq.	%	Freq.	%	Difference (%)	*p*
Percentage larger for two-year institutions						
Internships	34	56.7	60	20.9	35.8	***
Financial aid	20	33.3	31	10.8	22.5	***
Academic advising	40	66.7	160	55.7	11.0	
Service-learning	19	31.7	73	25.4	6.3	
Summer bridge program	5	8.3	8	2.8	5.5	*
Early-alert systems	28	46.7	120	41.8	4.9	
Peer mentoring by sophomores	18	30.0	83	28.9	1.1	
Common reading	4	6.7	16	5.6	1.1	a
Outdoor or wilderness adventure	3	5.0	12	4.2	0.8	a
Percentages larger for four-year institutions						
Major exploration and selection	7	11.7	108	37.6	-25.9	***
Live-on-campus requirement	2	3.3	72	25.1	-21.8	a
Living-learning community	1	1.7	56	19.5	-17.8	a
Career exploration	26	43.3	157	54.7	-11.4	
Study abroad	9	15.0	69	24.0	-9.0	
Peer mentors for sophomores	3	5.0	40	13.9	-8.9	a
Undergraduate research	7	11.7	58	20.2	-8.5	
Student government	8	13.3	60	20.9	-7.6	
Back-to-school event	10	16.7	71	24.1	-7.4	
Sophomore-specific residential curriculum	1	1.7	24	8.4	-6.7	
Online communication	9	15.0	60	20.9	-5.9	
Print publication	1	1.7	21	7.3	-5.6	a
Summer newsletter	1	1.7	19	6.6	-4.9	a
Retreats	3	5.0	27	9.4	-4.4	a
Class events	15	25.0	83	28.9	-3.9	
Faculty or staff mentors	12	20.0	67	23.3	-3.3	
Leadership development	23	38.2	117	41.1	-2.9	
Credit-bearing course	6	10.0	36	12.5	-2.5	
Other	5	8.3	31	10.8	-2.5	
Academic coaching or mentoring	17	28.3	88	30.7	-2.4	
Opportunities to coteach	5	8.3	29	10.1	-1.8	
Support for high D/F/W courses	9	15.0	45	15.7	-0.7	
Career planning	29	48.3	140	48.8	-0.5	
Cultural enrichment	10	16.7	49	17.1	-0.4	
Learning communities	8	13.3	39	13.6	-0.3	

Note. The sum of the percentages is larger than 100% due to the ability of respondents to select more than one response.
ᵃAnalysis was not conducted due to cell counts less than five.* *p* < .05. ** *p* < .01. *** *p* < .001.

Table 8 displays the differences in reported frequencies of sophomore-specific initiatives based on institutional control. Public institutions more frequently provided academic advising ($p < .05$) and internship programs ($p < .01$) than private institutions. Conversely, private institutions more frequently offered class events ($p < .001$), an on-campus living requirement ($p < .001$), leadership development ($p < .01$), student government ($p < .01$), retreats ($p < .001$), and a sophomore-specific residential curriculum ($p < .05$) to second-year students than their public counterparts. Of interest among these differences is that public institutions were more likely to identify academic advising as a vehicle to support sophomores; however, more than half of all private institutions also reported advising. In addition, initiatives at private institutions tended to revolve around extracurricular activities, particularly those in the traditional domain of student affairs.

Characteristics of the Primary Sophomore-Year Initiative

Following the I-E-O conceptual framework (Astin, 1991), the NSSYI sought to determine which sophomore-year initiative, program, or service (i.e., environment [E]) reached the greatest number of students on campuses. Further, the survey attempted to gain a greater understanding of the predominant initiative by (a) identifying the most frequently reported primary sophomore initiatives; (b) developing a scheme for categorizing the many possible initiatives offered by colleges and universities; (c) determining the reach of the primary initiative across campuses; and (d) outlining the most common objectives for sophomore programs, both overall and for specific categories.

Predominant Sophomore-Year Initiative

Participating institutions were asked to indicate which sophomore-year initiative reached the highest proportion of students (i.e., predominant initiative). Table 9 on page 18 presents the distribution of responses for the 11 most frequently identified primary initiatives. Academic advising was the service selected by the greatest number of institutions (45.7%) by a substantial margin. To illustrate, academic advising was named by more than five times as many respondents than an on-campus living requirement for sophomores, the second-most frequently identified primary initiative. The preponderance of academic advising as the sophomore initiative with the greatest scope on campuses is not entirely surprising. First, it would be rare to find an institution where each student was not assigned an academic advisor. However, because slightly less than half of all institutions indicated academic advising was the predominant initiative, it suggests respondents were referring to a specific sophomore initiative carried out by advisors rather than the act of advising itself. Academic advising is also one of the areas where sophomore initiatives have the longest history (Keup et al., 2010). In addition, two of the most frequently identified institutional objectives named by respondents for sophomores are directly connected to advising: academic assistance and selection of a major. Thus, academic advising has the potential to reach a large number of students in ways that align with institutional goals for the sophomore year.

Institutional respondents were given the opportunity to identify sophomore-specific initiatives not included in the list of options. The primary programs listed among the other responses included study abroad, sophomore-centered events (e.g., a summit aimed at discussing issues pertinent to sophomores or social events such as a faculty and alumni dinner), tutoring, and career-related events. In addition, three institutions described comprehensive sophomore-year experience programs, such as a coordinated set of curricular and cocurricular experiences offered throughout the second year.

When the primary sophomore initiative is examined by disaggregating the data by institutional type, results show that academic advising is offered by the same proportion of two- and four-year schools (45.8% and 45.7%, respectively). Early-alert systems (11.9%) and internships (8.5%) were the second and third most frequently named sophomore success programs. In contrast, four-year institutions identified sophomore year on-campus living requirements (9.6%) and credit-bearing courses, such as sophomore seminars, (3.9%) as the predominant second-year initiatives following academic advising. Since institutions could only select one primary initiative, many of the categories had fewer than five responses; therefore, the chi-square analysis for difference by institutional type was not conducted.

Table 8

Sophomore-Specific Initiatives by Institutional Control (n = 336)

Sophomore initiative	Institutional control				Difference (%)	p
	Public		Private			
	Freq.	%	Freq.	%		
Percentages larger for public institutions						
Academic advising	108	62.4	84	51.5	10.9	*
Internships	55	31.8	35	21.5	10.3	**
Academic coaching or mentoring	57	32.9	42	25.8	7.1	
Learning communities	29	16.8	17	10.4	6.4	
Financial aid	28	16.2	18	11.0	5.2	
Undergraduate research	37	21.4	28	17.2	4.2	
Peer mentoring by sophomores	55	31.8	45	27.6	4.2	
Support for high D/F/W courses	28	16.2	22	13.5	2.7	
Print publication	13	7.5	9	5.5	2.0	
Summer bridge program	8	4.6	5	3.1	1.5	
Online communication	34	19.7	30	18.4	1.3	
Percentages larger for private institutions						
Class events	30	17.3	63	38.7	-21.4	***
Live-on-campus requirement	21	12.1	53	32.5	-20.4	***
Leadership development	59	34.1	78	47.9	-13.8	**
Student government	23	13.3	43	26.4	-13.1	**
Retreats	6	3.5	24	14.7	-11.2	***
Career exploration	86	49.7	94	57.7	-8.0	
Career planning	78	45.1	86	52.8	-7.7	
Major exploration and selection	53	30.6	62	38.0	-7.4	
Sophomore-specific residential curriculum	8	4.6	17	10.4	-5.8	*
Back-to-school event	37	21.4	43	26.4	-5.0	
Study abroad	36	20.8	41	25.2	-4.4	
Credit-bearing course	17	9.8	23	14.1	-4.3	
Cultural enrichment	27	15.6	31	19.0	-3.4	
Living-learning community	27	15.6	30	18.4	-2.8	
Faculty or staff mentors	36	20.8	38	23.3	-2.5	
Other	16	9.2	19	11.7	-2.5	
Early-alert systems	73	42.2	71	43.6	-1.4	
Peer mentors for sophomores	21	12.1	22	13.5	-1.4	
Opportunities to coteach	16	9.2	17	10.4	-1.2	
Service-learning	46	26.6	44	27.0	-0.4	
Common reading	9	5.2	5	5.5	-0.3	
Outdoor or wilderness adventure	7	4.0	7	4.3	-0.3	
Summer newsletter	10	5.8	10	6.1	-0.3	

Note. The sum of the percentages is larger than 100% due to the ability of respondents to select more than one response. * $p < .05$. ** $p < .01$. *** $p < .001$.

Table 9
Predominant Sophomore-Year Initiatives (n = 341)

Primary initiative	Freq.	%
Academic advising	156	45.7
Sophomore live-on-campus requirement	28	8.2
Early-alert systems	16	4.7
Other	14	4.1
Credit-bearing course	13	3.8
Academic coaching	11	3.2
Class events	10	2.9
Sophomore living-learning community	10	2.9
Career exploration	8	2.3
Major exploration	7	2.1
Service-learning	7	2.1

An investigation of the differences by institutional control revealed noteworthy patterns. First, while academic advising was the primary initiative identified most often by both public and private colleges and universities, public institutions reported it as the primary second-year program more frequently (52.4%) than did private campuses (39.1%). Early-alert systems (5.9%) and second-year, live-on-campus requirements (4.1%) followed in frequency among public institutions. Live-on-campus requirements (13.0%) and credit-bearing courses (4.3%) followed in frequency among private colleges and universities. As was the case for institutional type, no test for statistical significance was performed among these groups due to many primary initiatives with low numbers of responses.

Categories of Sophomore-Year Initiatives

The 2014 NSSYI asked institutions to identify which of 33 programs, services, or initiatives they offered to sophomore students to aid in their success. During the analysis of the responses, it became apparent that it would be useful to create a categorization schema for the types of initiatives offered to sophomores. This was done for two reasons: (a) to combine initiatives with similar purposes or scope and (b) to collapse the number of institutions offering similar types of initiatives for comparison. To this end, a categorization was developed that reduced the number from 33 unique types (plus multiple *other* reported initiatives) to 14 categories of sophomore-year initiatives. The present categorization was created by combining initiatives from the questionnaire that were conceptually or practically related. It further incorporated the initiatives named in the responses to the *other* categories from the questions asking for discrete and predominant sophomore-year initiatives on campuses.

Table 10 presents a concordance between the sophomore-year initiatives listed in the NSSYI and the created categories. It should be understood that this categorization schema was developed as a heuristic device to assist in the analysis and interpretation of the results. It is possible that others would arrange the initiatives in different ways, which would yield a different grouping. However, as results presented later in the report will illustrate, this arrangement of sophomore programs proved to be a useful way to group them.

Table 10

Concordance Between NSSYI and Sophomore-Year Initiative Categories

Sophomore-year initiative categories	NSSYI listed sophomore-year initiative
Academic advising	Academic advising
Residential initiatives	Residence life, sophomore live-on-campus requirement Residence life, sophomore-specific living-learning community Residence life, sophomore-specific residential curriculum
High-impact practices (HIPs)	Common reading Cultural enrichment Internships Learning communities Service-learning or community service Study abroad Undergraduate research
Major and career focused Initiatives	Career exploration Career planning Major exploration and selection
Academic support	Course-specific support for classes Academic coaching or mentoring Faculty or staff mentors Peer mentors for sophomores
Campus-based events	Back-to-school event Class events
Early-alert systems and retention	Early-alert systems
Curriculum or course-based	Credit-bearing course
Leadership development	Leadership development Opportunities to coteach Peer mentoring by sophomores Student government
Communication to sophomores	Summer newsletter or communication Online communications Print publication
Comprehensive sophomore-year experience	Derived from open-ended responses
Away-from-campus experiences	Outdoor or wilderness adventure Retreats
Financial aid and scholarships	Financial aid
Transition-focused initiatives	Summer bridge program

Note. Sophomore-year initiatives from open-ended responses were used to create the categories but do not appear in the table to conserve space and to avoid confusion.

Table 11 presents the distribution of the categories of primary sophomore-year initiatives. Despite combining other categories, academic advising was the most frequently reported category (45.7%). Following in incidence were residential initiatives (12.3%), HIPs (7.9%), and major and career-focused initiatives (6.5%). The remaining categories of initiatives were reported by fewer than 20 institutions each. The resulting analyses based on these categories focus on the four most frequent initiatives (i.e., academic advising, residential, HIPs, and major and career) since they had enough responses to yield meaningful comparisons.

Table 11
Primary Sophomore-Year Initiative Categories (n = 341)

Primary initiative category	Freq.	%
Academic advising	156	45.7
Residential initiatives	42	12.3
High-impact practices (HIPs)	27	7.9
Major and career-focused initiatives	22	6.5
Academic support	19	5.6
Campus-based events	17	5.0
Early-alert systems and retention	16	4.7
Curriculum or course-based	13	3.8
Leadership development	11	3.2
Communication to sophomores	6	1.8
Comprehensive sophomore-year experience	3	0.9
Away-from-campus events	3	0.9
Financial aid and scholarships	2	0.6
Transition-focused initiatives	0	0.0
Unknown	4	1.2

When disaggregating the number of responses for the four largest categories of primary initiatives by institutional type, there was virtually no difference in the rates at which two- and four-year campuses offered academic advising (45.8% and 45.7%, respectively) and major and career-focused initiatives (6.8% and 6.4%, respectively). However, four-year institutions more frequently (14.5%) offered residential initiatives than did two-year institutions (1.7%). This stands to reason as four-year institutions are much more likely to have residence halls on campus than two-year institutions. Conversely, two-year colleges offered HIPs (15.3%) as primary sophomore-year initiatives at twice the rate of their four-year counterparts (6.4%).

A comparison of the frequency of institutions reporting primary sophomore initiatives in these four categories by institutional control revealed a slightly different pattern. As noted earlier, academic advising was reported at a greater rate by public institutions (52.4%) than private campuses (39.1%). However, private institutions offered residential initiatives (18.0%) at nearly twice the rate of public colleges and universities (7.6%). There was no difference in the rates at which HIPs (8.2% public, 8.1% private) and major and career initiatives (6.5% public, 6.2% private) were offered.

Reach of Primary Sophomore-Year Initiative

To understand the impact of the primary sophomore-year initiative, respondents were asked to identify the proportion of students on campus who were reached. Figure 7 presents the percentage of students participating in the primary sophomore program. Overall, approximately two in 10 institutions included all sophomores. Nearly half (49.3%) reached 80% or more of second-year students. Four-year institutions were significantly more likely (p < .01) to contact greater numbers of sophomores through the primary initiative than two-year campuses (Figure 7).

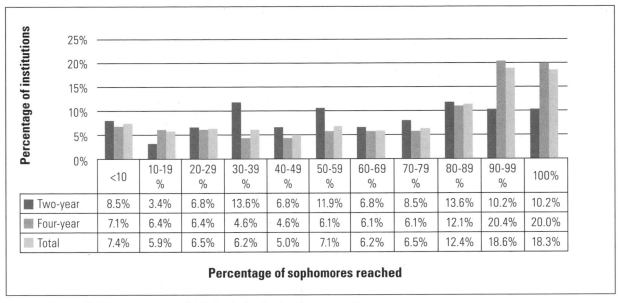

	<10	10-19 %	20-29 %	30-39 %	40-49 %	50-59 %	60-69 %	70-79 %	80-89 %	90-99 %	100%
■ Two-year	8.5%	3.4%	6.8%	13.6%	6.8%	11.9%	6.8%	8.5%	13.6%	10.2%	10.2%
■ Four-year	7.1%	6.4%	6.4%	4.6%	4.6%	6.1%	6.1%	6.1%	12.1%	20.4%	20.0%
▨ Total	7.4%	5.9%	6.5%	6.2%	5.0%	7.1%	6.2%	6.5%	12.4%	18.6%	18.3%

Percentage of sophomores reached

Figure 7. Reach of primary sophomore initiative by institutional type. *p* < .01.

Figure 8 shows the distribution of responses disaggregated by institutional control. Private colleges and universities were significantly more likely (*p* < .001) to contact greater numbers of students via their primary second-year programs than were public institutions. This result is interesting when contrasted with the finding that fewer private schools reported academic advising as the primary sophomore initiative. However, the percentage of private institutions reaching higher proportions of students is likely buoyed by the prevalence of campuses reporting sophomore live-on-campus requirements.

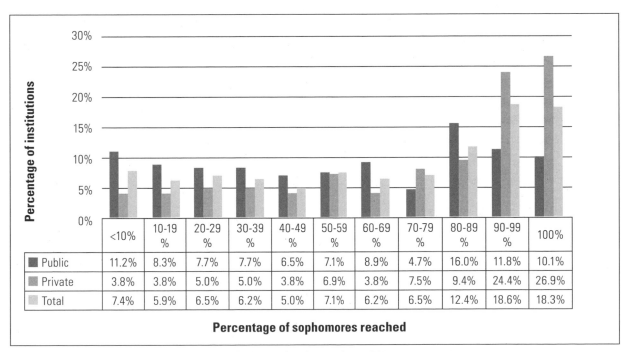

	<10%	10-19 %	20-29 %	30-39 %	40-49 %	50-59 %	60-69 %	70-79 %	80-89 %	90-99 %	100%
■ Public	11.2%	8.3%	7.7%	7.7%	6.5%	7.1%	8.9%	4.7%	16.0%	11.8%	10.1%
■ Private	3.8%	3.8%	5.0%	5.0%	3.8%	6.9%	3.8%	7.5%	9.4%	24.4%	26.9%
▨ Total	7.4%	5.9%	6.5%	6.2%	5.0%	7.1%	6.2%	6.5%	12.4%	18.6%	18.3%

Percentage of sophomores reached

Figure 8. Reach of primary sophomore initiative by institutional control. *p* < .001.

Required Participation in Primary Sophomore Initiative

Another way to understand the scope and desired impact of the primary initiative on campus is through the extent to which students are required to participate. Overall, four in 10 (40.3%) colleges and universities required 100% of their sophomores to participate in the primary second-year initiative. On the other end, one third of institutions did not require participation. Significantly more four-year institutions had a mandatory participation requirement for the primary sophomore initiative (43.4%) compared to two-year campuses (25.4%, $p < .01$). Similarly, private colleges and universities were significantly more likely to require all of their sophomores to engage with the primary initiative (51.9%) than public institutions (29.4%, $p < .001$). Overall, the sophomores most often required to participate in primary second-year initiatives were academically underprepared students (42.7%), first-generation students (34.1%), honors students (32.9%), international students (29.3%), and students participating in a learning community (26.8%).

When breaking down the requirement to participate by primary sophomore-year initiatives categories, noteworthy patterns are present. Among institutions where the primary initiative was academic advising, 60.4% of institutions required 100% of students to participate compared to 16.9% with no requirement. On campuses where academic advising was the primary program, students on probationary status (68.6%), academically underprepared students (51.4%), and undeclared students (51.4%) were more frequently required to participate. Thus, while most institutions with academic advising as the primary initiative required every sophomore to participate, there were many institutions that used advising as a tool to reach academically at-risk students.

Two in 10 (21.4%) campuses with primary residential initiatives also stipulated mandatory participation for all sophomores; 23.8% did not require it. Students in a particular residence hall (22.9%), learning-community participants (17.1%), and honors students (14.3%) were more frequently required to take part in residential initiatives. This suggests that while residential initiatives for sophomores were less likely to be mandatory, when they were, they were typically tied to a program, such as participation in a learning community or membership in an honors college.

A quarter (25.9%) of institutions offering HIPs as the predominant program required all sophomores to participate, where 29.6% required none. Students within specific majors (17.1%) and honors students (8.6%) were named more frequently as the groups required to participate by institutions with HIPs as the predominant initiative.

Institutions with major and career-focused primary initiatives were the least likely to call for mandatory sophomore participation (required, 9.1%; no requirement, 72.7%). Campuses with major and career-focused initiatives most frequently reported requiring students on probationary status (5.7%), undeclared students (2.9%), and learning community members (2.9%) to take part. While far fewer campuses with major and career-focused initiatives required students to participate, these initiatives targeted students at risk academically, similar to institutions with academic advising initiatives.

Objectives of the Primary Sophomore-Year Initiative

The objectives of the primary initiative can help understand the strategic vision institutions have for sophomores and highlight how they would like these students to develop. Overall, the five most frequent objectives for the primary sophomore-year experience were to (a) provide academic assistance (42.4%), (b) increase retention (42.4%), (c) improve students' connection with the institution (23.9%), (d) heighten student engagement (21.8%), and (e) strengthen graduation rates (19.7%).

Nonetheless, there were some differences in the objectives based on the category of the primary sophomore initiative (Table 12). As may be expected, each category had a fairly unique set of chief objectives. Institutions with HIPs and residential initiatives reported student engagement as their most frequently reported goal for sophomores. For major and career initiatives, the highest ranked objectives were career exploration and preparation, although HIP initiatives also considered these important. In addition, major and career initiatives, along with academic advising primary programs, identified graduation rates as a top goal. Of note, increasing student retention was represented in three of the four categories; however, it was not the primary objective of any group of initiatives.

Table 12

Most Frequently Reported Objectives by Top Four Categories of Primary Sophomore-Year Initiatives

	Percentage			
Objective	Academic advising (*n* = 152)	Residential initiatives (*n* = 40)	High-impact practices (*n* = 27)	Major and career-focused initiatives (*n* = 20)
Academic assistance	68.8			
Career exploration			18.5	57.1
Career preparation			18.5	38.1
Civic responsibility			22.2	
Connection with institution		62.5		
Critical-thinking skills			18.5	
Graduation rates	27.9			23.8
Intercultural competence			25.9	
Leadership opportunities			22.2	
Retention	51.9	45.0		28.6
Selection of a major	31.2			38.1
Self-exploration		22.5		
Student engagement		62.5	48.1	
Student-faculty interaction	17.5			
Support network		25.0		

Note. The five most frequent responses for each category of primary sophomore initiative reported; all other frequencies have been suppressed. The sum of the percentages is larger than 100% due to the ability of respondents to select more than one response.

Elements of HIPs in Sophomore-Year Initiatives

The Association of American Colleges and Universities (AAC&U), through their Liberal Education and America's Promise (LEAP) initiative, identified 10 high-impact practices (HIPs) where educational effectiveness has been demonstrated through numerous studies (Kuh, 2008). These HIPs include (a) first-year seminars and experiences, (b) common intellectual experiences, (c) learning communities, (d) writing-intensive courses, (e) undergraduate research, (f) collaborative assignments and projects, (g) diversity and global learning, (h) service-learning and community-based learning, (i) internships, and (j) capstone courses and projects. HIPs have been shown to yield increased benefits for a wide variety of students, especially those who come from groups who have historically been underrepresented in higher education (Kuh, 2008).

In a follow-up report describing how to ensure quality in HIPs and create new ones, Kuh (2013) identified eight key elements of high-impact practice: (a) performance expectations set at appropriately high levels; (b) significant investment of time and effort by students over an extended period of time; (c) interactions with faculty and peers about substantive matters; (d) experiences with diversity, wherein students are exposed to and must contend with people and circumstances that differ from those with which students are familiar; (e) frequent, timely, and constructive feedback; (f) periodic, structured opportunities to reflect and integrate learning; (g) opportunities to discover relevance of learning through real-world applications; and (h) public demonstration of competence. These conditions are hallmarks of quality educational environments and form the underlying basis for the benefits realized by HIPs.

The elements of high-impact practice provide a framework to identify ways the environment influences outcomes in effective ways. This is particularly important as HIPs have differential benefits for students who come from different backgrounds, namely improved outcomes for students from underrepresented groups. Moreover, many of the sophomore-year initiatives that were identified in previous administrations of the NSSYI were included in the 10 HIPs named by AAC&U (e.g., learning communities, undergraduate research, service-learning, internships). Using this framework facilitated an investigation of the educational effectiveness of sophomore-year initiatives. To that end, participants were asked to identify the extent to which each of the eight elements of high-impact practice was present in the predominant sophomore-year initiative. Respondents were given the opportunity to rate the presence of each element on a 5-point scale ranging from 1 = *element is not present* to 3 = *element is partially present* to 5 = *element is pervasive throughout*.

Table 13 demonstrates the overall proportion of institutions identifying the presence of high-impact practice elements in their primary sophomore-year initiatives. Seven of the eight elements were reported by 50% or more of all respondents as at least partially present in their predominant initiative. Approximately eight in 10 institutions report interactions with faculty and peers around substantive matters and performance expectations set at appropriately high levels as at least partially present in their primary sophomore programs. The only element named by fewer than half of all respondents as present in their primary initiative was public demonstration of competence. When the distribution of these responses was broken down by the institutional variables of type and control, no significant differences emerged.

Table 13

Extent of High-Impact Practice Elements in Primary Sophomore-Year Initiatives (n = 329)

Element	Freq.	%
Performance expectations set at appropriately high levels	259	78.7
Significant investment of time and effort by students over an extended period of time	227	69.0
Interactions with faculty and peers about substantive matters	267	81.2
Experiences with diversity, wherein students are exposed to and must contend with people and circumstances that differ from those with which students are familiar	194	59.0
Frequent, timely, and constructive feedback	242	73.6
Periodic, structured opportunities to reflect and integrate learning	216	65.7
Opportunities to discover relevance of learning through real-world applications	208	63.2
Public demonstration of competence	140	42.6

Note. Frequencies represent combined totals of responses rated 3 = *element is partially present* through 5 = *element is pervasive throughout*, on a 5-point scale.

When elements of high-impact practice were disaggregated by category of primary sophomore-year initiatives, noteworthy differences emerge. Table 14 displays the distribution of the reported presence of elements of educationally effective practice split out among the four most frequently named categories of primary sophomore initiatives.

The elements most frequently reported within academic advising included meaningful interactions with faculty and peers (82.9%) and performance expectations set at appropriately high levels (77.6%). Within residential initiatives, the most frequently cited elments were experiences with diversity (87.5%), meaningful interactions with faculty and peers (72.5%), and learning through real-world applications (72.5%). Investment of time and effort (96.3%) and learning through real-world applications (96.3%) were the top elements among institutions with HIPs as primary initiatives. Finally, institutions with major and career-focused primary initiatives most often named meaningful interactions with faculty and peers (65.0%) and performance expectations set at appropriately high levels (65.0%) as elements at least partially present.

Table 14
Extent of High-Impact Practice Elements in Top Four Categories of Primary Sophomore-Year Initiatives

Element	Academic advising (n = 152)		Residential initiatives (n = 40)		High-impact practices (n = 27)		Major and career-focused initiatives (n = 20)	
	Freq.	%	Freq.	%	Freq.	%	Freq.	%
Appropriately high performance expectations	118	77.6	27	67.5	25	92.6	13	65.0
Investment of time and effort	96	63.2	27	67.5	26	96.3	12	60.0
Interactions with faculty and peers	126	82.9	29	72.5	25	92.6	13	65.0
Experiences with diversity	65	42.8	35	87.5	22	81.5	9	45.0
Frequent, timely, and constructive feedback	113	74.3	21	52.5	24	88.9	12	60.0
Opportunities to reflect and integrate learning	94	61.8	27	67.5	24	88.9	9	45.0
Learning through real-world applications	83	54.6	29	72.5	26	96.3	11	55.0
Public demonstration of competence	55	36.2	14	35.0	21	77.8	4	20.0

Note. Frequencies represent combined totals of responses rated 3 = *element is partially present* through 5 = *element is pervasive throughout,* on a 5-point scale.

Perhaps not surprisingly, elements of educationally effective practices as described by Kuh (2013) were most prevalent in the initiatives representing HIPs. To reduce the potential of bias, the questionnaire asked respondents to identify the presence of *elements of educationally effective practices,* and did not refer to them as HIPs. Moreover, the initiatives included in the HIP category of predominant sophomore-year initiatives were each named individually. This convergence lends support to the notion that HIPs are high impact because of the presence of the elements outlined by Kuh (2010).

However, there is potential for high-impact practice in other types of sophomore-year initiatives. The presence of a majority of elements (five or more) were identified by at least 50% of institutions with academic advising, residential, and major and career-related initiatives. There is room for growth in these initiatives. One consistent finding was the element least frequently present in all initiatives was *public demonstration of competence.* It is likely less difficult to find ways in which students are already demonstrating competence in these programs than to create and add another component.

Conclusion

Sophomore issues continue to be a point of concern for many institutions of higher education across the United States. Nearly six in every 10 institutions reported some type of campuswide attention to sophomore students. This appears to be a growing trend, as most institutions that have included attention to sophomores in their institutional efforts (e.g., retention, assessment, strategic planning) have done so for five years or less.

Slightly fewer campuses (46.1%) reported offering at least one specific program, service, or initiative aimed at supporting sophomore students. This represents a steady growth in these programs over the three administrations of the NYSSI. Academic advising, career preparation, residential programs, and HIPs are the most frequently named initiatives. Objectives for sophomore initiatives include providing academic assistance, increasing retention, improving students' connection with the institution, heightening student engagement, and strengthening graduation rates. This demonstrates alignment with institutions' overall objectives for the sophomore year, such as year-to-year retention, career preparation and exploration, academic assistance, and selection of a major.

The NYSSI results highlight ways institutions have been providing initiatives that have natural and meaningful connections to institutional objectives for sophomores. In many instances, these initiatives have elements of educationally effective practice. Yet, unique institutional situations, necessities, and desired outcomes should guide the choices for how best to respond to sophomore student needs. In the I-E-O model (Astin, 1991), environment is a key piece in realizing desired student outcomes. The institutional environment should match the needs of each campus' specific sophomore population. Thereby, sophomore initiatives can serve as a high-impact practice leading to improved student success.

Sophomore Experiences Survey: Student Inputs and Outcomes

Each spring since 2007, the Sophomore Experiences Survey (SES), an online instrument administered by The Thriving Project at Azusa Pacific University, has been given to second-year students across the United States. The aim of the 2014 SES was to collect information about sophomore student thriving and to assess psychological sense of community, institutional integrity, spirituality, student-faculty interaction, and campus involvement among students in their second year of college. *Thriving* is conceptualized as optimal functioning in three key areas that contribute to student success and persistence: (a) academic engagement and performance, (b) psychological well-being, and (c) interpersonal relationships (Schreiner, 2010a). Thriving students invest effort to reach important educational goals; manage their time and commitments effectively; are engaged in the learning process; are optimistic about their future and positive about their present choices; are appreciative of differences in others; are committed to enriching their community; and connect in healthy ways to other people. They also function at optimal levels and gain maximum benefits from their college experience because they are psychologically engaged and involved in educationally productive behaviors.

Survey Instrument

The SES is an online instrument that assesses numerous indicators of student well-being, success outcomes, participation levels, interaction with peers and faculty, satisfaction, and entering characteristics. At the heart of the instrument is the Thriving Quotient (Schreiner, 2012), a 25-item measure of psychosocial well-being that incorporates five factors: (a) engaged learning, (b) academic determination, (c) social connectedness, (d) diverse citizenship, and (e) positive perspective. A confirmatory factor analysis conducted with 6,649 undergraduates in an earlier study yielded fit indices of $\chi2$ (123) = 651.15, p < .001; CFI = .954; TLI = .943; RMSEA = .053 with 90% confidence intervals from .049 to .057; CFI = .954; TLI = .943. Internal reliability of the instrument is strong, with a coefficient alpha of α = .89 and scale reliability estimates ranging from α = .74 to α = .88 (Schreiner, Kalinkewicz, McIntosh, & Cuevas, 2013).

Five other scales on the instrument were used to assess psychological sense of community, institutional integrity, spirituality, student-faculty interaction, and campus involvement. College students experience a sense of community when they are a part of a dependable network of relationships to which they contribute and feel as though they fit, matter, and belong (Lounsbury & DeNeui, 1995). This sense of community was measured by a four-item scale with a high level of reliability (α =.85). Institutional integrity (Braxton, Hirschy, & McClendon, 2004; α = .85) was measured with a three-item scale assessing students' perceptions of whether the institution was accurately portrayed at admission, faculty and staff actions and attitudes were consistent with the mission of the institution, and students' expectations were met. The spirituality scale was adapted from the Religious Commitment scale of the College Students Beliefs and Values survey (HERI, 2003) and was a reliable (α = .95) three-item construct assessing the extent to which students' spiritual or religious beliefs provided them with a sense of purpose and functioned as their foundation for life and for coping with difficult situations. An internally consistent (α = .86) student-faculty interaction scale, comprised eight items measuring the quality, quantity, and type of students' experiences with faculty. Lastly, campus involvement was measured by a reliable (α = .81) seven-item scale that assessed students' involvement in campus activities and organizations, including Greek and ethnic organizations, as well as their community service and leadership involvement.

Survey Administration

The survey was targeted at second-year students who were enrolled in degree-granting undergraduate institutions of higher education in the United States in spring of 2014. Recruitment began at the institutional level. All chief academic officers from accredited postsecondary institutions in the United States with contact information listed in the *Higher Education Directory* received an e-mail from the National Resource Center for The First-Year Experience and Students in Transition inviting them to participate in a national study of sophomore programs and administer the SES to their sophomores. Two additional follow-up e-mails were sent to remind institutions of the opportunity to participate in the study.

Administration of the survey was conducted throughout the spring of 2014. Once an institution agreed to participate, the designated contact person on campus was sent a custom URL to the weblink hosting the survey for their institution. The contact person then e-mailed each sophomore on campus with the URL and requested he or she complete the survey. No individual identifiers were on the survey, no IP addresses were collected, and students indicated their informed consent by proceeding to the second page of the survey. Further, this study had been determined to be exempt from full board review by the Institutional Review Board of Azusa Pacific University, the home of the Thriving Project.

In the spring of 2014, 24 institutions had sophomore response rates sufficient to be included in the data analysis. A total of 24,722 students were sent the SES by a contact person at their institution, and 4,450 submitted complete questionnaires, for a response rate of 18%. Because universities' institutional research offices typically selected sophomores to receive the survey based on their accumulated credit hours, students were also asked if this was their second year of college. It was found that 14.3% of the students in the sample were classified as sophomores by their institutions but were not in their second year of college; therefore, they were eliminated from further data analyses in order to gain a clearer picture of the second-year experience, leaving 3,643 second-year students in the final sample.

Participants

Table 15 presents the characteristics of the institutions that participated in the SES. Twelve of these institutions were public and 12 were private, with a broad representation of Carnegie types, size, selectivity, and geographic location. Two of the participating institutions were historically Black colleges or universities. Further, only one two-year college took part in the survey. This is a limitation of the study as the findings almost universally apply to four-year and predominantly White campuses. Moreover, the fact that only one two-year institution participated underscores the difficulty of defining sophomores in this context. It also highlights an opportunity for further research to better understand second-year students' experiences in community colleges. Appendix B presents the list of participating institutions that have given permission to include their names.

Of the 3,643 students in the sample, 2,535 were in public institutions, 935 were in private institutions, and 3,384 (92.9%) were between the ages of 18 and 20 years old. Table 16 on page 30 outlines the participants' demographic characteristics. There was a significantly higher percentage of African American students in the private institutions and a significantly higher percentage of Latino/a students in the public institutions. In addition, transfer students were a higher percentage of the public institution sample. Other than these demographic differences between the private and public institutions, there were no other significant differences in the two samples. Because regression analyses indicated that the type of institution was not a significant predictor of any of the outcome variables, all data analyses were conducted on the full sample. As with most online surveys, White students and females were overrepresented; therefore, the results of all data analyses are weighted by gender and race.

Table 15
Characteristics of SES Respondent Institutions (N = 24)

Institutional characteristic	%
Institutional control	
Public	50.0
Private	50.0
Selectivity	
Admits upper 10% of high school class	20.8
Admits upper 25% of high school class	33.3
Admits upper 50% of high school class	29.2
Open admissions	16.7
Carnegie classification	
Baccalaureate—diverse or arts and sciences	33.3
Master's – medium or larger programs	37.5
Research university – high or very high	29.2
Geographic location	
Northeast	20.8
Southeast	37.5
Central	29.2
West	12.5

Analyses

Analyses of the sample data were conducted at several levels. Frequency and descriptive statistics were carried out for each item and presented in the aggregate. Further, items of interest were disaggregated by student demographics, such as gender and race. Where appropriate, analysis of variance (ANOVA) was used to examine the differences in the means of various variables of interest between different groups of students. To better understand the predictive ability of student characteristics and experiences on outcomes of interest, such as thriving and student success, multiple linear regression techniques were used. Where comparisons yielded statistically significant differences, those are noted throughout the section.

The findings from the 2014 administration of the SES are organized around five research questions:

- To what extent is there sophomore slump, as evidenced by reported dissatisfaction, disengagement, lack of motivation, lower grades than in the first year, or perception that the sophomore year is worse than their first year?
- Are there gender or racial differences in levels of thriving, both as scale scores and as self-reported levels of overall thriving?
- To what extent do sophomores' levels of thriving predict other student success outcomes, such as their satisfaction, GPA, and intent to graduate from the institution?
- What is the contribution of sophomore programs to student success in regard to the variation in thriving, satisfaction, intent to graduate, perception of tuition worth, and institutional fit, after controlling for entering student characteristics?
- What are the demographic variables and campus experiences that are most predictive pathways to thriving for sophomore students?

While most questions from the instrument will receive treatment in this report, the national norms for all responses to the SES are presented in Appendix E.

Table 16
Demographic Characteristics of the Sophomore Sample (N = 3,643)

Characteristic	%
Gender	
Female	71.6
Male	28.4
Race	
African American	10.6
Asian	5.6
Caucasion/White	66.8
Latino/a	7.7
Multiethnic	6.3
Native American/Alaskan Native	1.6
Did not respond	1.4
Transfer student	
No	86.9
Yes	13.1
Annual household income	
Less than $30,000	15.7
$30,000 - $59,999	22.0
$60,000 - $89,999	24.0
$90,000 - $119,999	16.6
More than $120,000	13.5
Did not respond	8.2
Degree aspirations	
None	1.3
Bachelor's degree	28.5
Master's degree	45.4
Doctorate	16.0
Medical or law degree	8.9
Residence	20.8
On campus	53.5
Off campus	46.5
Work	12.1
Does not work	34.9
Works on campus	23.9
Works off campus	32.6
Works both on and off campus	8.6
Enrolled in the Honors Program on campus	5.8
No	88.3
Yes	11.7
First-generation student	
Yes	23.2
No	76.8

Sophomore Slump

Kennedy and Upcraft (2010) have characterized the sophomore slump as a multidimensional phenomenon that includes at least one of the following: (a) academic deficiencies, (b) academic disengagement, (c) dissatisfaction with the collegiate experience, (d) major and career indecision, and (e) developmental confusion. The results of the SES indicate that about 20% of the sophomores in this study would be categorized as slumping, and of additional concern, 27.3% reported they were surviving, barely surviving, or not surviving. Figure 9 presents the proportion of students indicating dissatisfaction or disengagement in key areas indicative of this slump.

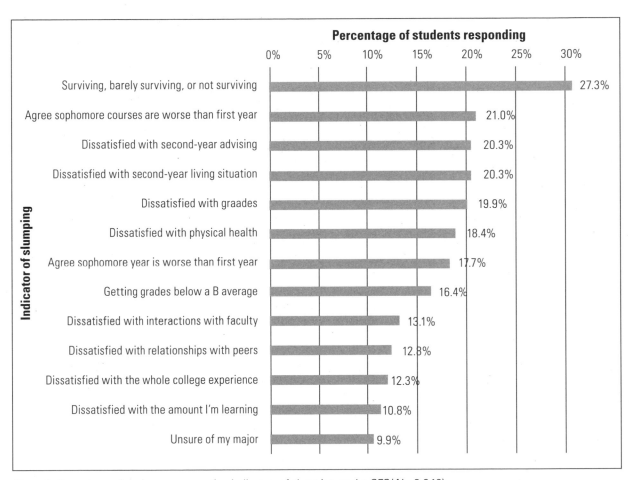

Figure 9. Percentage of sophomores reporting indicators of slumping on the SES (N = 3,643).

An examination of students' comments in response to an open-ended survey question revealed that sophomores described this experience as a loss of purpose and motivation, a lack of excitement, and a sense of loneliness and invisibility as the collective attention of the institution shifted to the next incoming class. Other second-year students seemed to expect this slump, noting there are numerous forks in the road during their journey through college in terms of decision making for the future and that the "sophomore year is when you finish all the crappy stuff, so I expected this." Students also realized they had a long road ahead of them, commenting that "we aren't new anymore, but we aren't getting out anytime soon, either!"

The overall results indicate that approximately 80% of sophomores report experiencing their second year as about the same or better than their first year, but based on their actual scores on the Thriving Quotient, only 19.4% are thriving when that is defined as scores of 5 or higher on a 6-point scale. The scale of thriving where students score highest is academic determination ($M = 4.82$); lowest scores are on the positive perspective scale ($M = 4.07$). When students are provided with the definition of thriving as *getting the most out of your college experience, so that you are intellectually, socially, and psychologically engaged and enjoying the college experience*, 39.8% describe themselves as thriving most of the time or consistently thriving (scores of 5 or higher on a 6-point scale). Thus, students tend to perceive themselves as thriving to a greater degree than indicated by their actual levels of engaged learning, academic determination, social connectedness, positive perspective, and diverse citizenship scores. Students who scored high in academic determination; social connectedness; and, especially, a sense of community (PSC) were most likely to rate themselves as thriving, suggesting that students' perceptions of thriving are primarily a combination of academic and interpersonal levels of well-being.

If approximately 20% of second-year students are consistently thriving and another 20% are barely surviving, the remaining 60% in the middle appear to be having a mixed experience on campus. That is, some things are going well for them, and other things are not going as well. Typically, these students listed specific events, both positive and negative, that affected their ability to thrive. It is this group that perhaps offers the most opportunity for interventions to enhance their thriving and ultimate success.

Gender and Racial Differences

To explore whether there were significant gender and racial differences in thriving or in the predictors of thriving, a number of statistical analyses were conducted. First, ANOVA was carried out to assess differences across groups within the dataset. Initial calculations explored gender differences. Table 17 outlines the mean scores on each scale of the Thriving Quotient for males and females, with significant differences noted. Statistically significant differences were found between men and women students on their total Thriving Quotient scores and three of the five scale scores (i.e., engaged learning, academic determination, and diverse citizenship), but not in their self-perception of whether they were thriving.

In addition, there were significant differences in all of the student success outcome variables except those related to finances (Table 17). For example, women reported higher levels of spirituality, a stronger sense of community on campus, greater certainty about their major, greater campus involvement, and higher levels of satisfaction with institutional integrity. There were no gender differences in students' perceptions of their second year being better or worse than their first, or in their participation in sophomore programming. There were no gender differences in students' frequency of interaction or satisfaction with faculty, except that women students were less likely than men to report having academic discussions with faculty. However, women students were more likely to meet with faculty during office hours, and men were more likely to interact informally and socially with faculty. Women students were also significantly more likely to see their advisor during their sophomore year.

Racial differences were observed in total Thriving Quotient scores, as well as all five thriving scales: institutional integrity, psychological sense of community, student-faculty interaction, campus involvement, and spirituality (Table 17). However, the differences were not consistent across racial groups; that is, in some cases, White students responded differently from all other students, while in other instances, the differences were between Asian students and all others, Latino/a students and all others, or African American students and all others. There were a number of patterns of concern, however. Asian students reported the lowest levels of thriving (Asian $M = 4.35$, Non-Asian $M = 4.48$; $p = .017$) and sense of community on campus (Asian $M = 4.45$, Non-Asian $M = 4.70$; $p = .004$), significantly lower than any other group. African American students in this sample were more involved on

Table 17

Analysis of Variance Between Gender and Ethnic Groups on Dependent Variables

| | Gender | | | | | Ethnic groups | | | | | Overall | |
| | Male (n = 933) | | Female (n = 2,389) | | | White (n = 2,552) | | Non-White (n = 770) | | | (n = 3,322) | |
Variable	M	SD	M	SD	p	M	SD	M	SD	p	M	SD
Thriving Quotient	4.42	0.62	4.50	0.60	**	4.48	0.59	4.46	0.64		4.48	0.60
Campus involvement	2.74	1.17	2.97	1.16	***	2.79	1.08	3.28	1.33	***	2.90	1.16
Engaged learning index	4.50	0.98	4.59	0.89		4.58	0.88	4.50	1.03		4.56	0.92
Academic determination	4.76	0.77	4.85	0.73	*	4.83	0.71	4.79	0.84	*	4.82	0.74
Diverse citizenship	4.65	0.80	4.83	0.70	***	4.75	0.70	4.86	0.81	***	4.78	0.73
Positive perspective	4.08	0.93	4.09	0.90		4.08	0.91	4.13	0.89		4.09	0.91
Social connectedness	4.10	0.97	4.14	1.04		4.16	1.03	4.01	0.99	***	4.13	1.02
Spirituality	4.01	1.38	4.30	1.31	***	4.10	1.34	4.60	1.26	***	4.22	1.34
Psychological sense of community	4.58	0.99	4.74	0.96	***	4.71	0.96	4.65	1.01		4.79	0.97
Institutional integrity	4.40	1.00	4.51	0.98	*	4.51	0.97	4.38	1.04	**	4.48	0.99
Faculty-student interaction	3.75	1.07	3.79	1.07		3.73	1.04	3.93	1.16	***	3.78	1.07

*$p < .05.$ **$p < .01.$ ***$p < .001.$

campus (African American M = 3.60, Non-African American M = 2.93; p = .000) and interacted most with faculty (African American M = 4.10, Non-African American M = 3.72; p = .000); however, their perceptions of institutional integrity (African American M = 4.34, Non-African American M = 4.50; p = .003) were lowest of any group.

After determining that racial group differences existed among many of the variables, hierarchical multiple regression models were developed for each ethnic group to assess the extent to which demographic characteristics, student inputs, and campus environment variables predicted thriving among each group of students. Distinct regression models were developed for African American, Latino/a, and Asian students. The regression model for Asian students was modified due to the limited sample size for this group. Regression analysis was chosen because the block effect of the analysis allows researchers the ability to isolate the distinct contribution made by the predictor variables within each block to the variability in the outcome variable. Blocks used for analysis were consistent with previous thriving literature and build upon Astin's (1991) I-E-O framework of inputs, environment, and outcomes.

A combination of attendance at sophomore-specific programs and campus involvement was a modestly significant contributor to the variation in thriving for African American students, as can be seen in block 5 of Table 18. However, the contribution of campus involvement was a negative predictor of thriving for these students; that is, African American students who reported higher levels of involvement on campus reported lower levels of thriving. Attendance at sophomore-specific events in and of itself did not contribute significantly to thriving for any of the groups explored.

Table 18
Hierarchical Multiple Regression Analysis Predicting Thriving of Ethnic Groups (n = 3,028)

Predictor variable	African American (n = 305) β	Latino/a (n = 230) β	Asiana (n = 171) β	White (n = 2,322) β
Block 1				
High school GPA	-.01*	-.10*	a	-
% female campus	-.09*	-	-	-.04**
Grad school bound	-	-	a	.05**
First enrollment choice	-	-	a	-
Household income	-	-	-	-
R² change	**.05**	**.06**	**.01**	**.04**
Block 2				
Private institution	-.13*	-	-	-
R² change	.00	.02	a	.00
Block 3				
Transfer	-	-	a	-
Athlete	-	-	a	-
Works on or off campus	-	-	-	.03*
Lives on campus	-	-	-	-
R² change	**.01**	**.04**	**.01**	**.01**
Block 4				
Spirituality	.32***	.26***	.20***	.18***
R² change	**.26**	**.18**	**.16**	**.13**
Block 5				
Campus involvement	-.12*	-	-	-
Sophomore programs	-	-	-	-
R² change	.02	.01	.02	.04
Block 6				
Faculty interaction	.23***	.16**	.19**	.15***
College GPA	-	.13**	-	.07***
Number of courses dropped	-	-.11*	a	-.04**
Service-learning	-	-	-	-
Learning community	-	-	-	.04**
Major certainty	-	.16***	-	.11***
Met with advisor	-	-	-	.04*
R² change	.10	.12	.16	.10
Block 7				
Institutional integrity	.11*	-	-	.13***
Financial difficulty	-	-	-	-.03*
R² change	**.11**	**.11**	**.10**	**.14**
Block 8				
PSC	.47***	.43***	.55***	.42***
R² change	.09	.08	.12	.08
Total ΔR²	**.62**	**.63**	**.58**	**.53**

Note. PSC = Psychological Sense of Community. Only those regression weights that were statistically significant at block 8 are included in the table.
ᵃ The model for Asian students differs from the other models because of sample size; therefore, it is one block smaller than the others and includes fewer variables.
* $p < .05$. ** $p < .01$. *** $p < .001$.

A distinction of note among the regression models explored is the degree that spirituality contributed to the variation in thriving among students of color. Spirituality contributed more to thriving among students of color than White students; it had the largest effect for African American students. These findings are consistent with previous explorations of spirituality and thriving among students of color (McIntosh, 2015).

Other Student Success Outcomes

A hierarchical multiple regression model was created to assess the extent to which thriving contributed to the variation in students' intent to graduate, institutional fit, overall satisfaction, perception of tuition as a worthwhile investment, and the likelihood they would choose their university again if they had the decision to do over. As indicated by the change in the R^2 levels in Block 6 of Table 19, after controlling for institutional differences, students' entering characteristics, amount of campus involvement, and degree of interaction with faculty, students' levels of thriving contributed an additional 6% to 14% to the variation in these outcomes. Levels of thriving explained the greatest amount of variance in students' overall satisfaction with the college experience, their perception of institutional fit, and their perception of tuition as a worthwhile investment.

High school GPA remained the strongest predictor of students' GPA in their second year followed by the number of courses dropped and thriving levels. Thriving also contributed an additional 8% to the variation in sophomores' intent to graduate, after taking into consideration campus experiences and students' precollege characteristics. Thus, thriving appears to operate as a mediating variable between specific campus experiences and student success outcomes. To the extent that such experiences have a positive effect on students' engaged learning, goal direction and investment of effort, social connectedness, openness to differences, civic engagement, and positive perspective, they affect students' levels of success.

Table 19
Hierarchical Multiple Regression Analysis of Student Success Outcomes (n = 2,987)

Predictor variable	Intent to graduate β	Overall satisfaction β	Tuition is worthwhile investment β	Institutional fit β	Would choose institution again β
Block 1					
African American	.03*	-	-	-	-.03*
Asian	-	-	-	-	-
Latino/a	-	-	-	-	-
Female	-	-	-	-	-
High school GPA	.05**	-	-	-	-
First generation	-	-	-	-	-
First enrollment choice	.05**	-	.05***	.05**	.13***
Household income	-	-	-	-	-
Degree aspirations	-	-	-	-	-
R² change	.04	.03	.05	.05	.08
Block 2					
Transfer	-	-	-	-	-
Athlete	-.04*	-.03*	-	-	-
Works on or off campus	-	-	-	-	-
Lives on campus	.05***	-	.04**	.04**	.04*
R² change	.01	.00	.00	.00	.00
Block 3					
Spirituality	-	.03*	.05*	-	-
R² change	.01	.04	.04	.04	.01

Table 19 continues on page 36

Table 19 continued from page 35

Predictor variable	Student success criterion variables				
	Intent to graduate β	Overall satisfaction β	Tuition is worth-while investment β	Institutional fit β	Would choose institution again β
Block 4					
Campus involvement	-	-	-	-	-
Sophomore programs	.13***	-	.05**	.05*	.09***
R² change	**.04**	**.03**	**.01**	**.01**	**.01**
Block 5					
Faculty interaction	-	.09***	-	-	.04*
College GPA	-	-	-	-	-
Number of courses dropped	.05**	-.04**	-	-	.04*
Service-learning	-	-	-	-	-
Learning community	-	-	-	-	-
Major certainty	.07***	.06***	.09***	.08***	.06***
Met with advisor	.05***	-	.04**	.04**	-
R² change	**.04**	**.07**	**.06**	**.06**	**.02**
Block 6					
Thriving Quotient M	-	.10***	-	.04*	-
R² change	**.08**	**.14**	**.12**	**.14**	**.06**
Block 7					
Institutional integrity	.09***	.34***	.20***	.20***	.13***
Financial difficulty	-	-	-.03*	-	-.04*
R² change	**.05**	**.17**	**.14**	**.13**	**.08**
Block 8					
PSC	.43***	.32***	.51***	-	.44***
R² change	**.07**	**.04**	**.11**	**.10**	**.08**
Total ΔR²	**.29**	**.33**	**.51**	**.51**	**.33**

Note. PSC = Psychological Sense of Community. Only those regression weights that were statistically significant at block 8 are included in the table.
* $p < .05$. ** $p < .01$. *** $p < .001$.

Contribution of Sophomore Programs to Student Success

Although the impact of sophomore programming on the variation in student success outcomes is difficult to determine without an experiment that randomly assigns students to a treatment or control condition, preliminary evidence can be determined from the data collected in this study. The online survey asked students to indicate how often they had participated in any campus program or service that was geared specifically to sophomores. Their responses were entered into a hierarchical multiple regression analysis after the institutional characteristics and student demographic characteristics, which were statistically controlled. This analysis indicated that sophomore programs were a small, but statistically significant, predictor of student success outcomes, such as the intent to re-enroll or graduate, perceived institutional fit, and perception that tuition was a worthwhile investment, as well as significantly predictive of the levels of thriving among White and African American students, but not among Asian or Latino/a students. Sophomore programming particularly contributed to the thriving scales of diverse citizenship, social connectedness, and academic determination (Table 19 above). It appeared as though students who were most likely to be involved on campus were also those most likely to participate in sophomore programming; thus, there may be a selection bias operating in those students who choose to participate in sophomore programs. However, this preliminary indication of the contribution of sophomore programs is an important element to consider in student success in the second year. The types of sophomore programs in which students participated was not known, so further study is needed to determine the impact of particular programs.

Given that advising was the type of sophomore programming most often described by institutional representatives who responded to the NSSYI, particular attention to students' perceptions of advising and to the role that advising played in their success and thriving is warranted. Students were asked to indicate how frequently they saw their advisor and how satisfied they were with the advising they received. Among the total sample of sophomores, more than 43% met with their advisor regularly or frequently, and 78.7% were satisfied with that experience. These percentages are considerably higher than seen in previous iterations of the SES dating back to 2007. Of continuing concern, however, are the 17.3% who rarely or never met with their advisor, as well as the 21.3% who were dissatisfied with the advising experience. A content analysis of student comments on the survey revealed that negative remarks about advising outweighed positive ones and typically focused on inaccurate advice, lack of knowledge about programs, or no help in determining a major. Because sophomores' satisfaction with advising was highly correlated with their overall satisfaction with faculty and the entire college experience, as well as their perception that tuition was a worthwhile investment, continued attention to the advising experience in the second year is warranted, particularly as major and career decisions are of paramount concern for students during this time.

Pathways to Thriving

The final research question examined the campus experiences and pathways that were most predictive of sophomore thriving among all students. To explore this relationship, a hierarchical multiple regression analysis was conducted on the total sample which included students' precollege characteristics; initial campus experiences; levels of spirituality; engagement on campus; academic indicators; financial difficulty and perceptions of institutional integrity; and psychological sense of community on campus (Table 20).

Table 20
Hierarchical Multiple Regression Analysis of Thriving Sum Scores and Scale Scores (n = 2,994)

	Thriving Quotient scores					
Predictor variable	Engaged learning β	Academic determination β	Social connected-ness β	Diverse citizenship β	Positive perspective β	Total Thriving Quotient score β
Block 1						
African American	.03*	.04*	-	-	-	-
Asian	-	-	-	-	-	-
Latino/a	-	-	-	-	-	-
Female	-	.03*	.04*	.04*	.05**	.03*
High school GPA	-	.08***	-	-.04*	-	
First generation	-	-	-	-	-	
First enrollment choice	-	-	.04*	-	-	-
Household income	-.04*	-	-	-	-	-
Degree aspirations	.05**	.05**	-	.08***	-	.05**
R² change	**.03**	**.06**	**.02**	**.05**	**.01**	**.04**
Block 2						
Transfer	-	-	-.05**	-	-	-
Athlete	-	-	.04*	-.04*	-	-
Works on or off campus	-	.03*	.06***	-	-	.04**
Lives on campus	-	-	.07***	-	-	-
R² change	**.00**	**.01**	**.00**	**.00**	**.00**	**.01**
Block 3						
Spirituality	.09***	.14***	-	.22***	.23***	.19***
R² change	**.01**	**.04**	**.04**	**.04**	**.01**	

Table 20 continues on page 38

Table 20 continued from page 37

Predictor variable	Thriving Quotient scores					
	Engaged learning β	Academic determination β	Social connected-ness β	Diverse citizenship β	Positive perspective β	Total Thriving Quotient score β
Block 4						
Campus involvement	.11***	.05*	.11***	.14***	.06***	.04**
Sophomore programs	-	.04*	.11***	-.09***	-	.11***
R^2 change	**.01**	**.01**	**.02**	**.05**	**.01**	**.03**
Block 5						
Faculty interaction	.23***	.15***	.16***	-	-	.15***
College GPA	.07***	.18***	-	,04*	-	.07***
Number of courses dropped	-.04**	-.05**	-	-	-.06**	-.04*
Service-learning	-	-	-	-	.04*	
Learning community	.03*	-	-	.04**	-	.03*
Major certainty	.12***	.15***	-	-	.06***	.10***
Met with advisor	-	.05**	.06***	-	.04**	.04**
R^2 change	**.12**	**.13**	**.02**	**,05**	**.02**	**.10**
Block 6						
Institutional integrity	.12***	.07***	-	.09***	.11***	.11***
Financial difficulty	-	-	-.05*	-	-	-
R^2 change	**.10**	**.06**	**.05**	**.08**	**.04**	**.10**
Block 7						
PSC	.35***	.33***	.33***	.35***	.17***	.42***
R^2 change	.06	.05	.05	.06	.01	.08
Total ΔR^2	**.38**	**.38**	**.19**	**.44**	**.20**	**.53**

Note. PSC = Psychological Sense of Community. Only those regression weights that were statistically significant at block 7 are included in the table.
* $p < .05$. ** $p < .01$. *** $p < .001$.

Conclusion

Based on the data collected from the second-year students who participated in the 2014 SES, it appears that the academic, social, and psychological well-being inherent in the construct of thriving mediates the effect of campus experiences on such student success outcomes as GPA, perception that tuition is worthwhile, institutional fit, intent to graduate, and whether the student would choose the institution again. That is, campus experiences designed to enhance student success have a greater effect when they increase students' levels of thriving. Those who design and implement such campus opportunities for sophomores would benefit from ensuring that the experiences (a) engage students in learning, (b) connect them in healthy ways to others and to the larger community, (c) expose them to differences and ways of valuing difference in others, and (d) bolster their academic and psychological coping skills.

The sense of community sophomores experience on campus, as well as their perceptions of institutional integrity, play a major role in their ability to thrive in the second year. Feelings of belonging and ownership, combined with opportunities to work synergistically with others, celebrate successes, and receive support during difficult times, are bolstered when the institution as a whole delivers on its promises. This experience, in turn, leads students to engage further and to participate on campus in ways that enhance their ability to succeed.

Discussion

The two research projects described in this report, the 2014 administrations of the NSSYI and SES, provide insight into the practices and outcomes related to interventions and conditions that lead to sophomore student success. As a thorough discussion of each previously presented result is not practical, this section highlights selected findings and implications of the same. This discussion draws on the I-E-O (Astin, 1991) model to present a framework for integrating and discussing the results of the two studies. In particular, it begins by focusing on the connection of sophomores' background characteristics (i.e., inputs) to outcomes. It then turns to the link between sophomore environments to outcomes, particularly around sense of community and educationally effective practices. This is followed by further discussion of student outcomes and environments, specifically sophomore-year initiatives. The discussion concludes with an interrogation of the concept of the sophomore slump and how better understanding its indicators can point to more targeted student success initiatives, programs, and services. Suggestions for improving the sophomore-year experience on campuses and recommendations for future research are also presented.

Outcomes Based on Background Characteristics

Several of the SES analyses revealed differences in second-year student behaviors and outcomes based on background characteristics of the students, particularly by race and ethnicity as well as gender.

Race and Ethnicity

The four major pathways to thriving in the sophomore year, defined on the SES, were (a) campus involvement, (b) student-faculty interaction, (c) spirituality, and (d) a sense of community. However, it is important to note the extent to which these pathways contribute to thriving in the sophomore year varied greatly by ethnic or racial group. Ethnic minority students had fewer pathways to thriving than majority students on predominantly White campuses; those pathways differed across ethnic groups, as well. For example, campus involvement was a significant pathway to thriving for White students, but its benefits for students of color were less clear. Among African American students, campus involvement had little effect on their thriving unless the student was in a leadership role. For Latino/a and Asian students, participating in campus events and organizations did not contribute to the variation in their thriving. Further examination of SES data revealed there were major hurdles to campus involvement among underrepresented students: for Latino/a students, commuter status was the biggest obstacle to campus engagement, and for African Americans, it was working off campus. Moreover, Latinos/as were the most likely to be commuters, and African American students were the most likely to work off campus for 20 hours a week or more.

An examination of student-faculty interaction also revealed a different pattern for underrepresented students than for majority students on predominantly White campuses. Overall, the level of interaction and satisfaction with faculty was the only specific campus-experience variable that significantly predicted not only thriving but every positive student success outcome for sophomores. However, there were racial differences in the degree to which faculty interaction helped students succeed and thrive. For example, African American students reported interacting with faculty more than any other racial group but benefited the least from that interaction. Their interactions were least likely to be positive or rewarding, yet when these students had positive interactions, that experience contributed more to their ability to thrive than was evident in any other racial group. Asian students interacted the least with faculty, although Latino/a students also reported little interaction.

Spirituality was the pathway to thriving that was significantly stronger in underrepresented students than in majority students on predominantly White campuses. Levels of spirituality were twice as predictive of thriving among students of color as among White students. These effects were most pronounced among African American students, for whom spirituality was the major predictor of their thriving. For students of color, and African American students in particular, spiritual or religious beliefs seemed to serve as an anchor and source of support that enabled them to navigate a predominantly White campus successfully.

Although these three pathways to thriving (i.e., campus involvement, student-faculty interaction, and spirituality) represent the campus experiences that may be of primary benefit for students to get the most out of their college experience, by far the strongest contributor to thriving in the second year was the extent to which sophomores experienced a psychological sense of community. First described by Sarason in 1974, this sense of community has been defined by McMillan and Chavis (1986) as "a feeling that members have of belonging and being important to each other, and a shared faith that their needs will be met by their commitment to be together" (p. 9). Students, faculty, and staff who report a strong sense of community on campus feel they are part of a stable and dependable network of people who care about them, are committed to their growth and well-being, and are able to meet their needs (Lounsbury & DeNeui, 1995).

Among sophomores in the SES study, 34.8% *agreed* or *strongly agreed* there was a strong sense of community on campus, and only 5.1% reported a very low score on this scale; the remaining students had scores that ranged from *somewhat disagree* to *somewhat agree* in describing their sense of community on campus. White students were significantly more likely to report a strong sense of community on campus than were students of color, with the lowest scores reported by Asian students. Taken together, these findings indicate potentially fruitful areas for campus attention to the needs of underrepresented students so that the collegiate experience, particularly in the critical second year, can have the intended impact on all students.

Gender

On the SES, women reported greater levels of sense of community, satisfaction with institutional integrity, campus involvement, academic determination, diverse citizenship, spirituality, and overall thriving. In addition, women were more likely to see their advisor during the sophomore year. However, there were no differences by gender in engaged learning, positive perspective, social connectedness, student-faculty interaction, perception of the second year being better or worse than the first, or participation in sophomore programming. These results suggest that, overall, women appear to be somewhat better off in terms of thriving in the sophomore year, although gender did not emerge as a strong predictor. The study findings warrant further investigation to understand how gender differences in thriving and perception of the second year influence students' overall approach to college. Results from such research would point to opportunities to deliver support and programming to better support men and women in the second year of college.

Connecting Environments to Outcomes

The findings from the SES provided evidence for the importance of environments in the student success equation. While participation in sophomore programs was not a consistent predictor of student success outcomes or thriving, sense of community and institutional integrity were consistently among the strongest predictors.

Sense of Community

Sense of community was the single strongest positive predictor of all student outcomes on the SES. Similarly, this was one of the most frequently reported objectives of predominant sophomore-year initiatives by respondents to the NSSYI. Overall, when students reported higher academic determination, social connectedness, and sense of community on campus, they were more likely to report thriving. This is consistent with previous research that found when sophomores discover purpose on campus, they are more likely to be motivated (Graunke & Woosley, 2005; Schreiner, 2010b), an important aspect of thriving. Additionally, academic and social integration were named by Tinto (1975), in his seminal theory on student departure, as important antecedents to institutional and goal commitment, essential ingredients to college student success.

Thus, as institutions continue to focus on sophomore student success, higher education professionals should ask, How can we help sophomores feel like they are an important part of campus? One approach is to consider the ways in which sophomores' needs are similar yet different from those of first-year students. Academic support is still critical for second-year students, but their concern has likely shifted from the how (e.g., How can I find success in all of these classes?) to the why (e.g., Why am I taking all these classes?). Students' sense of belonging may also be shifting from questioning whether their institution is a good fit to how that college or university fulfills their sense of purpose. Sophomores are moving from finding a place to fit in to finding a place where they have a sense of community—academically and socially. The two domains traditionally discussed separately start to converge around the idea of meaning, mattering, and purpose in college and beyond.

Demonstrating Institutional Integrity

Sense of community was measured as a psychological construct in the SES; however, it is influenced by, and largely dependent on, the external environment. Further, it is through the efficacy of educational programs where institutions make good on the promises made in viewbooks, during campus tours, and throughout orientation. Institutions striving to realize the lofty promises of educational achievement are more likely to do so as they incorporate elements of high-impact practice into their student success programs. The high-impact practice element most frequently reported overall on the NSSYI was interactions with faculty and peers about substantive matters, followed by appropriately high performance expectations and frequent, timely, and constructive feedback. The most often reported types of sophomore programs included academic advising and initiatives focused on career and majors, such as one-on-one interaction between a student and an educator. This suggests most institutions recognize, to some extent, those interactions become more than transactional exchanges and are critical educational opportunities. However, the high-impact elements least frequently reported were public demonstration of competence, experiences with diversity, and opportunities to make real-world applications of learning. These point to areas where institutions can work to deliver on the educational promises they have made to students.

Analysis of student responses to the SES indicate that participation in sophomore programs was positively linked to intent to graduate and whether students would choose the institution again. These are consistent with several of the most frequently identified objectives for sophomore-year initiatives on the NSSYI, including increasing retention, strengthening graduation rates, and improving students' connection with the institution. Moreover, participation in sophomore programming strongly contributed to diverse citizenship, social connectedness, and academic determination. These conditions of thriving are also linked to frequently named objectives, such as connection with the institution and student engagement. Yet, more information is needed to understand the unique impact of different types of sophomore programming and, even further, the role the delivery of elements high-impact practices plays in achieving desired outcomes for sophomore students.

Outcomes of Sophomore-Year Initiatives

The NSSYI identified four groups of sophomore-year initiatives reaching the greatest number of students on campuses: (a) academic advising, (b) residential initiatives, (c) HIPs, and (d) major and career-focused initiatives. Each type of initiative has the potential to improve students' sense of community and perception of the integrity of the institution.

Academic Advising

Academic advising, the most commonly identified sophomore-year initiative on campuses, is a natural place for institutions to deliver on their objectives to provide academic assistance and strengthen retention and graduation rates. Keup et al. (2010) referred to academic advising as "the most underestimated characteristic of a successful sophomore-year experience" (p. 32). Since most institutions require each student to have an academic advisor, this becomes a critical leverage point for increasing sophomore student success.

Sophomores need to select a major, find an academic home, and understand what the institution requires of them to graduate. However, a notable minority (17.3%) of students in the SES reported rarely or never meeting with their advisor. Of those who did, one fifth reported dissatisfaction with the experience. Moreover, a majority of comments about the quality of the advising included complaints about inaccurate advice, lack of knowledge about programs, or failure to help students select a major. This is a critical concern as the advising relationship carries incredible potential as a HIP for students, particularly in the sophomore year. Sophomore satisfaction with advising was highly correlated with overall satisfaction with the institution, including the value of tuition as a worthwhile investment.

Gordon (2010) suggested that advising sophomores requires special knowledge and competencies and that training programs should be offered to staff working with this population. Among her recommendations for second-year student advisors were (a) facilitating reflection on the first year's academic experience, (b) making plans for graduation, (c) discussing academic skills and habits, (d) identifying long-term academic and career opportunities, (e) encouraging ongoing cocurricular engagement, and (f) working with students who are still undecided or are considering changing majors. We echo these recommendations. The academic advising appointment has incredible potential to go beyond a transactional meeting and to contribute to the student's sense of academic and social belonging on campus.

Effective advising can be a cornerstone for designing a sophomore program. Advising for the second year needs to begin late in the first year so students can prepare for the challenges they will face as sophomores. Although advising models differ between campuses, using institutional data is critical in understanding any student cohort. Leveraging offices of institutional research, registrars, or other campus resources should be a strategy to ensure advisors have an informed perspective on any incoming sophomore advisee to better address second-year concerns.

Residential Initiatives

A substantial number of institutions identified a residential initiative as the sophomore-specific program that reached the greatest number of students on campus. Residence halls have developed over time to deliver an increasing array of cocurricular educational experiences. Respondents to the NSSYI reported offering sophomore-specific living-learning communities and residential curricula as well as requiring students to live in on-campus housing during their second year. The most frequently cited objectives for residential initiatives included developing a connection with the institution, fostering student engagement, supporting retention, cultivating a support network, and encouraging student self-exploration. Student responses to the SES provide evidence to suggest these objectives are being met for sophomores who live on campus. Living in an on-campus residence hall was a significant and positive predictor of social connectedness, intent to graduate, tuition as a worthwhile investment, sense of institutional fit, and satisfaction with institutional choice. It is important to note that while significant, these were not strong predictors. Further, there is a possibility sophomores who live on campus have chosen that option and may have done so because they have a strong sense of connection to the institution. More research is warranted to isolate and understand the impact of on-campus living in the second year toward meeting these goals.

To continue supporting sophomore-year initiatives in the residence halls, Gahagan and Hunter (2010) recommended gathering information about the students who live on campus, examining the institutional policy climate for second-year students, reconceptualizing the roles of resident assistants, building in assessment, and integrating the academic experience into sophomores' places of residence. As housing departments set out learning models or residential curricula, we challenge professionals to consider how the curriculum can extend beyond the needs of first-year students and provide a foundation to an educationally purposeful sophomore-year residential experience.

High-Impact Practices

Respondents to the NSSYI identified six of the 10 AAC&U HIPs (Kuh, 2008) as the sophomore-year initiative on campus reaching the largest proportion of second-year students: (a) common intellectual experiences (represented by common reading programs), (b) learning communities, (c) undergraduate research, (d) diversity and global learning (cultural enrichment and study abroad), (e) service learning, and (f) internships. Most commonly, these HIPs were offered to students to increase their engagement. Institutions also reported developing intercultural competence and civic responsibility as objectives for these sophomore-year initiatives. The SES only asked students to report their participation in two HIPs: learning communities and service-learning. Involvement in learning communities was a significant positive predictor of engaged learning and diverse citizenship as well as overall thriving. In addition, students who enrolled in a service-learning course had greater ratings of positive perspective.

Campus professionals who choose to implement HIPs as sophomore year initiatives should also concern themselves with the quality of these programs. The simple addition of a program or educational activity that has been identified by name as a HIP does not guarantee its effectiveness. The purposeful inclusion of the elements of high-impact practices as outlined by Kuh (2013) can give these sophomore initiatives the best chance for success. This may be happening now as evidenced by the finding that HIPs were the sophomore initiative with the greatest reported presence of educationally effective practice; however, these results point to avenues for future research. Further studies should examine the quality of the HIP under consideration to have a more complete understanding of the conditions leading to the benefits of participating in these practices.

Major and Career-Related Initiatives

Many respondents on the NSSYI described initiatives in which sophomores' major and career concerns were supported together in a single program. Overall, institutions with major or career-related initiatives reported career exploration and preparation and selection of a major as their primary objectives. Major certainty was a significant and positive predictor of all student success measures and overall thriving among respondents to the SES. This lends support to earlier findings stating that, perhaps, the most important decisions made during the second-year are solidifying a course of study, a major, and making plans for a career path after graduation (Coburn & Treeger, 1997; Gahagan & Hunter, 2006; Gardner, 2000). Finding this focus and sense of direction and purpose leads to greater motivation and subsequent success during the second year (Graunke & Woosley, 2005; Schreiner, 2010b). Schreiner, Nelson, and Louis (2012) recommended that campus programs be designed from a long-term viewpoint, including life beyond college, in order to provide perspective for important transition points, such as major or career choice.

Academic advisors, career service professionals, and other providers of sophomore-specific initiatives should carefully evaluate the ways in which they might work in coordinated and complementary ways to help students understand how decisions made now connect to longer term goals. Interventions with this focus can provide clarity and force sophomores to wrestle with difficult but developmentally appropriate and necessary issues.

Sophomores: Slumping? Thriving? Something Else?

College students face unique challenges during the sophomore year. This is a time when they are expected to select a major leading to a career path and an academic home on campus. Much commentary has pointed to the potential difficulty for sophomores in finding their academic and social footing. Sophomores who participated in the SES reported a more nuanced picture of how they are coping with these challenges. Approximately 20% of students stated they were thriving. Conversely, somewhere between 20% and 30% of them experienced a slump, leaving a substantial proportion (50-60%) of students falling somewhere between thriving and surviving. These findings suggest a multiplicity of approaches are likely required to support sophomores, depending on whether they are thriving, slumping, or in the middle.

Designing sophomore success programs for students who are slumping is perhaps the most straightforward. These students are often easily identified on campus through behavioral struggles, low grades, requests for academic support services, or undeclared major status. Institutional recognition of this group's need for support was evident in the responses to the NSSYI, where students with lack of academic preparation, probationary status, and an undeclared major were among the most frequently required to participate in the primary sophomore success initiative on campus. In these cases, it is easy to match the student need to the objective. For example, academically underprepared students were more frequently required to participate in academic advising while students who had not declared a major were more frequently required to engage in major and career-related initiatives.

Sophomores who are thriving have many assets on which student success programs can build. Thriving students are academically motivated and have high self-concept, direction, motivation, and engagement. As thriving was largely predicted by such things as spirituality, faculty interaction, major certainty, institutional integrity, and sense of community, programs that continue to provide opportunities for development in these areas are best poised to continue to support student thriving in the second college year.

Interestingly, the sophomores in the SES study presented some contradictory information about their overall well-being. Nearly eight in 10 respondents reported their second year was about the same or better than their first year. Yet, when considering the overall thriving quotient, only two in 10 were thriving. This disconnect between student self-perception and actual need can present challenges to faculty and staff who are tasked with supporting sophomore student success. Overall, only 40% of colleges and universities in the NSSYI required all sophomores to participate in the primary sophomore success initiative. This suggests that for the majority of sophomore initiatives, the decision to participate is left up to the student. If 80% of students feel the second year is equal to or better than the first year, they may believe they have achieved success and be less inclined to participate in programs.

The middle group of students—those who fall somewhere between thriving and slumping—are the most difficult to reach. They are the largest group of sophomore students, and if they do not believe they need extra services because they are not struggling, they can remain invisible by choice. In open-ended responses to the NSSYI, many institutions reported they did not have current sophomore programs because earlier initiatives were discontinued due to lack of students' interest or perceived need. As noted above, a large percentage of sophomores may believe they have transitioned the first college year successfully and do not need further institutional support. Yet, retention figures suggest otherwise, since it is not only slumping students, by our definition, who are leaving college. It is natural, given these findings, for those responsible for attending to second-year student success to ask, How do I convince sophomore students they need this specific support that will ultimately lead to success? Perhaps the question that higher education professionals should be asking is, How do I infuse highly effective programs that will meet the needs of our sophomore students into the existing institutional culture? Rather than trying to establish the value proposition to draw the average sophomore into a program or office, these students can be offered meaningful and high-impact opportunities throughout the curriculum and in services they are already required to use, such as academic advising or career exploration and planning.

Additional Recommendations for Practice

Throughout this discussion, practical suggestions have been offered to improve specific sophomore outcomes. However, given the fiscal constraints at colleges and universities across North America, any new campus initiative will exist in an ever-tightening budgetary climate. Designing an effective sophomore program requires an understanding of that institution's unique student population so money can be strategically shifted or allocated for new initiatives. Developing a sophomore profile and matching it to campus initiatives and opportunities is a good way to identify gaps, opportunities, and useful current sophomore programs. Any effective intervention strategy is informed primarily by the context in which it will exist. Creating a successful sophomore program requires a fulsome understanding of first-to-second-year retention, the experiences of second-year students on campus, and existing campus programs that are working well.

Building on effective programs means expanding already successful campus initiatives, with a specific focus on sophomores. Second-year students should find themselves unable to avoid opportunities to take part in HIPs, residential initiatives, career and vocational counseling, and targeted academic advising. Any new programs must be embedded in the student experience, which requires an understanding of where students exist on campus so the initiative becomes a part of the regular routine of the students it intends to serve. Creating such environments demonstrates institutional integrity and contributes to a sense of community on campus, important predictors of student thriving and success.

Future Directions for Research

While the two parallel research projects discussed in this report have produced valuable information about the prevalence, structures, and types of initiatives developed for sophomores as well as student characteristics, engagement, and outcomes, there is still much to learn about the second college year. The NSSYI and SES have created pathways for future research to understand the connection between institutional action and student development.

One avenue worth exploring is whether institutional objectives are being met vis-à-vis student outcomes. Conducting the NSSYI and SES in parallel facilitated a better understanding of the influence of institution-level decisions (e.g., primary sophomore-year initiative) on student-level outcomes (e.g., overall thriving). Future analyses of the data collected by these surveys will employ multilevel modeling techniques to connect student and institutional variables. This approach will allow us to discuss the institutional conditions affecting students in a variety of ways.

More work is needed to decipher the influence of background characteristics, such as gender and race, in students' participation in particular sophomore-year initiatives. Further, connecting participation rates of specific populations of students (e.g., African Americans, women) to student outcomes can point to programs and services that are promising for these groups of sophomores. Moreover, these results would have particular importance for institutions that serve large numbers of these students, such as historically Black colleges and universities or women's colleges. Qualitative studies using methods such as narrative analysis or case study can delve into the personal stories of individuals who have found success in the second year and help identify promising practices for working with specific populations, such as underrepresented minorities, men, and first-generation students.

Because of the high incidence of institutions reporting academic advising as the sophomore initiative with the greatest reach, a better understanding of the advising experience is required. This research could include descriptive statistics of the timing of sophomore advising as well as time spent in each meeting, interpretive studies examining the advising relationship from both the advisor and student perspectives, case studies pointing to successful approaches to advising, and experimental designs comparing a transactional advising experience (i.e., focus on fulfilling degree requirements and the mechanics of registration) with one that includes educationally effective practices (e.g., structured opportunities to reflect and integrate learning, interactions with faculty about substantive matters, opportunities to discover relevance of learning through real-world applications).

Further research is also warranted to improve understanding of the influence of HIPs on student success measures, such as thriving. Such research could expand the number of HIPs students would be able to report as engagements beyond learning communities and service-learning. Additionally, future studies should examine the effect of the varying quality of HIPs, or other programs with elements of high-impact practice, and their connection to sophomore student success.

Finally, more needs to be done to understand the unique sophomore experience in two-year colleges. Many of the studies of sophomores have been conducted on four-year campuses and describe the developmental processes of full-time college students in the traditional age range. Future research should examine the second-year experience for part-time, working students to explore how their status as a student mixed with other responsibilities shapes their sophomore year. A phenomenological or grounded theory study could present a rich description of the phases or processes that are salient to a variety of students at two-year colleges. Further, the very notion of the sophomore year may be a privileged construct; studies using a critical theoretical framework may shed light on improved approaches in environments where that construct does not hold up.

Conclusion

The data gathered through each of these instruments, the NSSYI and SES, contributes to the national picture of the practice and influence of institutional attention to the second year. Thereby, the information presented in this report can serve as a comparative tool, particularly when disaggregated by institutional or student characteristics. The results can be used by institutions to create initiatives targeted at clearly defined pathways to sophomore student success. It is our hope these findings will urge institutions to consider student inputs when shaping educational environments aimed at well-reasoned outcomes.

Appendix A: Survey Instrument: 2014 National Survey of Sophomore-Year Initiatives

Instructions

This survey is intended to gather information regarding sophomore-year initiatives on your campus. The survey should take approximately 20 minutes to complete. While you may exit the survey at any time and your responses will be saved, we recommend completing the entire survey in one sitting.

Specifically, you will be asked questions regarding the following:
- General institutional information
- Institutional attention to sophomores
- Coordination of institutional efforts
- Types of programs offered to sophomores
- Characteristics of the predominant sophomore-year initiative
- Educationally effective practices
- Administration
- Assessment and evaluation

For the purposes of this survey, we offer the following definitions:

Campus or Institution: These terms, used interchangeably, refer to an individual campus that is either (a) an independent entity or (b) meaningfully distinct from other campuses in a system.

Sophomores: Students in their second year at the same campus (excluding transfer students). These students may not have attained official standing based on accumulated credits.

Sophomore-Year Initiative: Any educational offering *specifically* or *intentionally* geared toward sophomore students. You can find a list of examples of sophomore-year initiatives here.

If you would like a copy of your responses, you will need to print each page of your survey before moving on to the next page.

Your responses are important to us, so please complete this survey by May 31, 2014. Thank you.

Institutional Information

Q1. Your first name:

Q2. Your last name:

Q3. Your title:

Q4. Your e-mail address:

Q5. Full name of institution:

Q6. City:

Q7. State:

Q8. Please indicate the category that best describes your institution's type:

- ❑ Two-year
- ❑ Four-year

Q9. Please indicate the category that best describes your institution's control:

- ❑ Public
- ❑ Private, not-for-profit
- ❑ Private, for-profit

Q10. What is the total undergraduate enrollment at your institution?

- ❑ Fewer than 500 students
- ❑ 501-1,000 students
- ❑ 1,001-1,500 students
- ❑ 1,501-3,000 students
- ❑ 3,001-5,000 students
- ❑ 5,001-10,000 students
- ❑ 10,001-15,000 students
- ❑ 15,001-20,000 students
- ❑ More than 20,000 students

Institutional Attention to the Sophomore Year

Q11. Which of the following institutional efforts have included a specific focus on the sophomore year? (Select all that apply.)

- ❑ Accreditation
- ❑ Institutional assessment
- ❑ Grant-funded project
- ❑ Participation in a national survey
- ❑ Program self-study
- ❑ Retention study

❏ Strategic planning

❏ Other, please specify:_____

❏ Our institution has not engaged in any efforts with a specific focus on the sophomore year. *[Go to Q15]*

Q12. How long have your institutional efforts included a specific focus on the sophomore year?

❏ 1 year or less

❏ 2-5 years

❏ 6-10 years

❏ 11-15 years

❏ 16-20 years

❏ More than 20 years

Q13. Which of the following campuswide objectives has your institution created specifically for the sophomore year? (Select all that apply.)

❏ Academic assistance

❏ Academic skills

❏ Career exploration

❏ Career preparation (e.g., internships, co-ops)

❏ Civic responsibility

❏ Connection with the institution

❏ Critical-thinking skills

❏ Financial literacy

❏ Graduation rates

❏ Information literacy

❏ Institutional resources and information

❏ Intercultural competence

❏ Leadership opportunities

❏ Oral communication skills

❏ Preprofessional preparation (e.g., premed, prelaw)

❏ Retention

❏ Selection of a major

❏ Self-exploration or personal development

❏ Service-learning

❏ Student engagement

❏ Student satisfaction

❏ Student-faculty interaction

❏ Study skills

❏ Support network or friendships

❒ Writing skills

❒ Other, please specify:_____

❒ Our institution has not created campuswide objectives specifically for the sophomore year.

Current Sophomore-Year Initiatives

Q14. Does your institution currently offer any initiatives specifically or intentionally geared toward sophomore students?

❒ Yes [Go to Q20]

❒ No

❒ I don't know.

Q15. Please indicate the reason(s) why your institution does not have a sophomore initiative: (Select all that apply.)

❒ Lack of expertise

❒ Lack of funding

❒ Lack of staff or faculty buy-in

❒ Limited time

❒ Not an institutional priority

❒ Other, please specify: _____

Past Sophomore-Year Initiatives

Q16. Has your institution had initiatives specifically or intentionally geared toward sophomore students in the past five years?

❒ Yes [Go to Q17]

❒ No [Go to Q18]

❒ I don't know. [Go to Q18]

Q17. Please indicate which of the following sophomore initiative(s) your institution had in the past five years: (Select all that apply.)

❒ Academic advising

❒ Academic coaching or mentoring

❒ Back-to-school events

❒ Career exploration

❒ Career planning

❒ Class events (i.e., trips, dinners, dances)

❒ Common reading experience

❒ Course-specific support for classes with high dropout, failure, or withdraw rates

❒ Credit-bearing course (e.g., sophomore seminar)

❒ Cultural enrichment activities (e.g., plays, musical events, multicultural fairs)

❒ Early-alert systems

❒ Faculty or staff mentors

❒ Financial aid (e.g., sophomore scholarships, loans)

- ☐ Internships
- ☐ Leadership development
- ☐ Learning communities (i.e., students take two or more linked courses as a group)
- ☐ Major exploration and selection
- ☐ Online communications (e.g., newsletters, social media)
- ☐ Opportunities to co-teach or assist in teaching a class
- ☐ Outdoor or wilderness adventure
- ☐ Peer mentoring by sophomores (i.e., sophomore students mentoring any other students)
- ☐ Peer mentors for sophomores (i.e., undergraduate students mentoring sophomores)
- ☐ Print publications (e.g., sophomore newsletters)
- ☐ Residence life—sophomore live-on-campus requirement
- ☐ Residence life—sophomore-specific living-learning community
- ☐ Residence life—sophomore-specific residential curriculum
- ☐ Retreats
- ☐ Service-learning or community service
- ☐ Student government (e.g., sophomore council)
- ☐ Study abroad
- ☐ Summer bridge programs
- ☐ Summer newsletters or communication
- ☐ Undergraduate research
- ☐ Other, please specify:_____

Future Sophomore-Year Initiatives

Q18. Is your institution considering or developing any future initiatives specifically or intentionally geared toward sophomore students?

- ☐ Yes *[Go to Q19]*
- ☐ No *[Go to Q48]*
- ☐ I don't know. *[Go to Q48]*

Q19. Please indicate which of the following future sophomore initiative(s) your institution is considering or developing: (Select all that apply.)

- ☐ Academic advising
- ☐ Academic coaching or mentoring
- ☐ Back-to-school events
- ☐ Career exploration
- ☐ Career planning
- ☐ Class events (i.e., trips, dinners, dances)
- ☐ Common reading experience
- ☐ Course-specific support for classes with high dropout, failure, or withdraw rates

- ❐ Credit-bearing course (e.g., sophomore seminar)
- ❐ Cultural enrichment activities (e.g., plays, musical events, multicultural fairs)
- ❐ Early-alert systems
- ❐ Faculty or staff mentors
- ❐ Financial aid (e.g., sophomore scholarships, loans)
- ❐ Internships
- ❐ Leadership development
- ❐ Learning communities (i.e., students take two or more linked courses as a group)
- ❐ Major exploration and selection
- ❐ Online communications (e.g., newsletters, social media)
- ❐ Opportunities to co-teach or assist in teaching a class
- ❐ Outdoor or wilderness adventure
- ❐ Peer mentoring by sophomores (i.e., sophomore students mentoring any other students)
- ❐ Peer mentors for sophomores (i.e., undergraduate students mentoring sophomores)
- ❐ Print publications (e.g., sophomore newsletters)
- ❐ Residence life—sophomore live-on-campus requirement
- ❐ Residence life—sophomore-specific living-learning community
- ❐ Residence life—sophomore-specific residential curriculum
- ❐ Retreats
- ❐ Service-learning or community service
- ❐ Student government (e.g., sophomore council)
- ❐ Study abroad
- ❐ Summer bridge programs
- ❐ Summer newsletters or communication
- ❐ Undergraduate research
- ❐ Other, please specify: _____ *[Go to Q48]*

Q20. In which of the following areas does your institution currently have initiatives specifically or intentionally geared toward sophomore students? (Select all that apply.)

- ❐ Academic advising
- ❐ Academic coaching or mentoring
- ❐ Back-to-school events
- ❐ Career exploration
- ❐ Career planning
- ❐ Class events (i.e., trips, dinners, dances)
- ❐ Common reading experience
- ❐ Course-specific support for classes with high dropout, failure, or withdraw rates

❒ Cultural enrichment activities (e.g., plays, musical events, multicultural fairs)

❒ Early-alert systems

❒ Faculty or staff mentors (i.e., faculty or staff mentoring sophomore students)

❒ Financial aid (e.g., sophomore scholarships, loans)

❒ Internships

❒ Leadership development

❒ Learning communities (i.e., students take two or more linked courses as a group)

❒ Major exploration and selection

❒ Online communications (e.g., newsletters, social media)

❒ Opportunities to co-teach or assist in teaching a class

❒ Outdoor or wilderness adventure

❒ Peer mentoring by sophomores (i.e., sophomore students mentoring any other students)

❒ Peer mentors for sophomores (i.e., undergraduate students mentoring sophomores)

❒ Print publications (e.g., sophomore newsletters)

❒ Residence life—sophomore live-on-campus requirement

❒ Residence life—sophomore-specific living-learning community

❒ Residence life—sophomore-specific residential curriculum

❒ Retreats

❒ Service-learning or community service

❒ Student government (e.g., sophomore council)

❒ Study abroad

❒ Summer bridge programs

❒ Summer newsletters or communication

❒ Undergraduate research

❒ Other, please specify: _____

Coordination of Sophomore-Year Initiatives

Q21. On your campus, how coordinated are sophomore-year initiatives? (Select the most appropriate answer.)

Totally decentralized, no coordination between any departments or units of sophomore-year initiatives				Totally centralized, all sophomore-year initiatives are coordinated by a single director or office	Don't know
1	2	3	4	5	DK

Q22. Please specify which campus units participate in the coordination of their sophomore-year initiatives: _____

Q23. Is there currently an individual in charge of sophomore student programs or initiatives?

- ❒ Yes *[Go to Q24]*
- ❒ No *[Go to Q28]*
- ❒ I don't know. *[Go to Q28]*

Q24. What is the title of the individual who is responsible for sophomore student programs or initiatives (e.g., director, coordinator, dean of sophomore student programs)? _____

Q25. Is this position dedicated to sophomore programs and initiatives on a full-time basis (approximately 40 hours per week)?

- ❒ Yes *[Go to Q28]*
- ❒ No *[Go to Q26]*
- ❒ I don't know. *[Go to Q26]*

Q26. Does this person have another position on campus?

- ❒ Yes *[Go to Q27]*
- ❒ No *[Go to Q28]*
- ❒ I don't know. *[Go to Q28]*

Q27. The other campus role of the dean, director, or coordinator of the sophomore initiative is as a/an: (Select all that apply.)

- ❒ Academic affairs administrator
- ❒ Faculty member
- ❒ Student affairs administrator
- ❒ Other, please specify:_____

Primary Institutional Initiative

Q28. Which of the following initiatives reaches the highest proportion of sophomore students at your institution? (Select only one.)

- ❒ Academic advising
- ❒ Academic coaching or mentoring
- ❒ Back-to-school events
- ❒ Career exploration
- ❒ Career planning
- ❒ Class events (i.e., trips, dinners, dances)
- ❒ Common reading experience
- ❒ Course-specific support for classes with high dropout, failure, or withdraw rates
- ❒ Credit-bearing course (e.g., sophomore seminar)
- ❒ Cultural enrichment activities (e.g., plays, musical events, multicultural fairs)
- ❒ Early-alert systems

❐ Faculty or staff mentors

❐ Financial aid (e.g., sophomore scholarships, loans)

❐ Internships

❐ Leadership development

❐ Learning communities (i.e., students take two or more linked courses as a group)

❐ Major exploration and selection

❐ Online communications (e.g., newsletters, social media)

❐ Opportunities to coteach or assist in teaching a class

❐ Outdoor or wilderness adventure

❐ Peer mentoring by sophomores (i.e., sophomore students mentoring any other students)

❐ Peer mentors for sophomores (i.e., undergraduate students mentoring sophomores)

❐ Print publications (e.g., sophomore newsletters)

❐ Residence life—sophomore live-on-campus requirement

❐ Residence life—sophomore-specific living-learning community

❐ Residence life—sophomore-specific residential curriculum

❐ Retreats

❐ Service-learning or community service

❐ Student government (e.g., sophomore council)

❐ Study abroad

❐ Summer bridge programs

❐ Summer newsletters or communication

❐ Undergraduate research

❐ Other, please specify: _____

You indicated the initiative reaching the highest proportion of sophomore students on your campus is [Insert response from Q28]. Please answer the following questions based only on this initiative.

The Students

Q29. What is the approximate percentage of sophomore students this initiative reaches on your campus?

❐ Less than 10%

❐ 10-19%

❐ 20-29%

❐ 30-39%

❐ 40-49%

❐ 50-59%

❐ 60-69%

❐ 70-79%

❒ 80-89%

❒ 90-99%

❒ 100%

Q30. What proportion of your second-year students are required to participate in this initiative?

❒ None are required to participate. *[Go to Question 32]*

❒ Less than 10%

❒ 10-19%

❒ 20-29%

❒ 30-39%

❒ 40-49%

❒ 50-59%

❒ 60-69%

❒ 70-79%

❒ 80-89%

❒ 90-99%

❒ 100% *[Go to Question 32]*

Q31. Which of the following groups of second-year students are required to participate in this initiative? (Select all that apply.)

❒ Academically underprepared students

❒ First-generation students

❒ Honors students

❒ International students

❒ Learning community participants

❒ Preprofessional students (e.g., prelaw, premed)

❒ Student athletes

❒ Students enrolled in developmental or remedial courses

❒ Students on probationary status

❒ Students participating in dual-enrollment programs

❒ Students residing within a particular residence hall

❒ Students with fewer credits than necessary for sophomore status

❒ Students within specific majors, please list: _____

❒ TRIO participants

❒ Undeclared students

❒ Other, please specify: _____

Q32. Which of the following groups of sophomore students are specifically targeted by this initiative? (Select all that apply.)

- ❏ Academically underprepared students
- ❏ Honors students
- ❏ International students
- ❏ Learning community participants
- ❏ Preprofessional students (e.g., prelaw, premed)
- ❏ Student athletes
- ❏ Students enrolled in developmental or remedial courses
- ❏ Students on probationary status
- ❏ Students participating in dual-enrollment programs
- ❏ Students residing within a particular residence hall
- ❏ Students with fewer credits than necessary for sophomore status
- ❏ Students within specific majors, please list: _____
- ❏ TRIO participants
- ❏ Undeclared students
- ❏ Other, please specify: _____

Characteristics of the Initiative

Q33. How long has this initiative been in place?

- ❏ 2 years or less
- ❏ 3-5 years
- ❏ 6-10 years
- ❏ 11-15 years
- ❏ 16-20 years
- ❏ More than 20 years

Q34. Please select the three most important objectives for this initiative:

- ❏ Academic assistance
- ❏ Academic skills
- ❏ Career exploration
- ❏ Career preparation (e.g., internships, co-ops)
- ❏ Civic responsibility
- ❏ Connection with the institution
- ❏ Critical-thinking skills
- ❏ Financial literacy
- ❏ Graduation rates
- ❏ Information literacy
- ❏ Institutional resources and information
- ❏ Intercultural competence

❐ Leadership opportunities

❐ Oral communication skills

❐ Preprofessional preparation (e.g., premed, prelaw)

❐ Retention

❐ Selection of a major

❐ Self-exploration or personal development

❐ Student engagement

❐ Student satisfaction

❐ Student-faculty interaction

❐ Study skills

❐ Support network or friendships

❐ Writing skills

❐ Other, please specify: _____

Educationally Effective Practices

Q35-42. To what extent are each of the following elements present in this initiative?

Element	Element is not present		Element is partially present		Element is pervasive throughout initiative
	1	2	3	4	5
Performance expectations set at appropriately high levels					
Significant investment of time and effort by students over an extended period of time					
Interactions with faculty and peers about substantive matters					
Experiences with diversity, wherein students are exposed to and must contend with people and circumstances that differ from those with which students are familiar					
Frequent, timely, and constructive feedback					
Periodic, structured opportunities to reflect and integrate learning					
Opportunities to discover relevance of learning through real-world applications					
Public demonstration of competence					

Administration of the Initiative

Q43. Which campus unit directly administers this initiative?

- ❏ Academic affairs central office
- ❏ College or school (e.g., College of Liberal Arts)
- ❏ Academic department(s), please specify: _____
- ❏ Second-year program office
- ❏ Student affairs central office
- ❏ Student affairs unit, please specify: _____
- ❏ Other, please specify: _____

Q44. How is the initiative *primarily* funded?

- ❏ Auxiliary funds—non-tuition-based fees and services (e.g., housing, bookstore)
- ❏ Foundation funds
- ❏ Grant funds
- ❏ Nonrecurring or one-time funds
- ❏ Recurring state- or university-appropriated funds
- ❏ Student activity fees
- ❏ Other, please specify: _____
- ❏ Assessment and Evaluation

Assessment and Evaluation

Q45. Has this initiative been formally assessed or evaluated in the past three years?

- ❏ Yes *[Go to Q47]*
- ❏ No *[Go to Q49]*
- ❏ I don't know. *[Go to Q49]*

Q46. What type of assessment was conducted? (Select all that apply.)

- ❏ Analysis of institutional data (e.g., GPA, retention rates, graduation rates)
- ❏ Direct assessment of student learning outcomes
- ❏ Focus groups
- ❏ Individual interviews
- ❏ Program review
- ❏ Student course evaluation
- ❏ A locally developed (i.e., home-grown) survey
- ❏ A national survey (e.g., CLA, IDEA, SSI) *[Go to Question 48]*

Q47. Please identify the national survey(s) you used: (Select all that apply.)

- ❐ College Student Experiences Questionnaire (CSEQ)
- ❐ Collegiate Learning Assessment (CLA)
- ❐ Community College Survey of Student Engagement (CCSSE)
- ❐ Faculty Survey of Student Engagement (FSSE)
- ❐ Individual Developmental and Educational Assessment (IDEA)
- ❐ National Survey of Student Engagement (NSSE)
- ❐ Second-Year Student Assessment (Noel-Levitz)
- ❐ Sophomore Experiences Survey (www.thrivingincollege.org)
- ❐ Student Satisfaction Inventory (SSI)
- ❐ Other, please specify: _____

Information

Q48. It is our practice to make available specific and general information gathered from this survey. In general, findings from the survey are reported in aggregate, but we may identify individual institutions that have agreed to allow their responses to be shared. Please select your preference:

- ❐ You may share my school's name and survey responses.
- ❐ Please do not share my school's name, but you may share my survey responses.
- ❐ Please do not share my survey responses.

Q49. It is our practice to create a research report based on an analysis of the general information gathered from this survey. Would you like to be informed when this research report is made available?

- ❐ Yes
- ❐ No

Appendix B: List of Institutions Participating in the 2014 National Survey of Sophomore-Year Initiatives and Sophomore Experiences Survey[a,b]

Institution	City	State
Alderson Broaddus College	Philippi	WV
American International College	Springfield	MA
Anna Maria College	Paxton	MA
Arapahoe Community College	Littleton	CO
Auburn University at Montgomery	Montgomery	AL
Bay de Noc Community College	Escanaba	MI
Bay Path College	Longmeadow	MA
Bennett College for Women	Greensboro	NC
Berry College	Mount Berry	GA
Bethany College	Lindsborg	KS
Bethune-Cookman University	Daytona Beach	FL
Big Bend Community College	Moses Lake	WA
Broome Community College	Binghamton	NY
Brown Mackie College-Louisville	Louisville	KY
Burlington County College	Pemberton	NJ
California Institute of the Arts	Valencia	CA
California State University-Channel Islands	Camarillo	CA
California State University-Northridge	Northridge	CA
Cape Fear Community College	Wilmington	NC
Castleton State College	Castleton	VT
Central State University	Wilberforce	OH
Chippewa Valley Technical College	Eau Claire	WI
Clemson University	Clemson	SC
College of Saint Benedict	Saint Joseph	MN
Columbia Basin College	Pasco	WA

[a]This is a partial list (n = 171) of total respondents to the National Survey of Sophomore-Year Initiatives (n = 778). Institutions were provided the opportunity to opt out of being publicly identified as a survey respondent.
[b]Participants in the Sophomore Experiences Survey have been marked with an asterisk (*). If an institution opted out of being identified in the NSSYI, they were not identified as a participant.

Institution	City	State
Columbia College	Columbia	SC
Columbus State University	Columbus	GA
Community College of Philadelphia	Philadelphia	PA
Concordia University-Portland	Portland	OR
Concordia University-Texas	Austin	TX
Coppin State University	Baltimore	MD
Cuyamaca College	El Cajon	CA
Delaware County Community College	Media	PA
Drake University	Des Moines	IA
Duke University	Durham	NC
East Carolina University	Greenville	NC
Eastern Florida State College	Cocoa	FL
Elizabeth City State University	Elizabeth City	NC
Elizabethtown College	Elizabethtown	PA
Elmhurst College	Elmhurst	IL
Elon University	Elon	NC
Emory University	Atlanta	GA
Flint Hills Technical College	Emporia	KS
Florida Atlantic University	Boca Raton	FL
Fort Peck Community College	Poplar	MT
Georgia Gwinnett College	Lawrenceville	GA
Georgia Institute of Technology-Main Campus	Atlanta	GA
Georgia Southern University	Statesboro	GA
Gordon State College	Barnesville	GA
Governors State University	University Park	IL
Graceland University-Lamoni	Lamoni	IA
Grayson College	Denison	TX
Helene Fuld College of Nursing	New York	NY
Indiana State University	Terre Haute	IN
Indiana University-Purdue University-Indianapolis	Indianapolis	IN
Inter American University of Puerto Rico-San German	San German	PR
J. F. Drake State Community and Technical College	Huntsville	AL
Kalamazoo College	Kalamazoo	MI
Kanawha Valley Community and Technical College	South Charleston	WV
Kaplan University-Mason City Campus	Mason City	IA
Keiser University-Ft Lauderdale	Fort Lauderdale	FL
Kent State University at Geauga	Burton	OH
Keweenaw Bay Ojibwa Community College	Baraga	MI
Keystone College	La Plume	PA
Lackawanna College	Scranton	PA
Lasell College	Newton	MA
Lawrence Technological University	Southfield	MI
Lehigh Carbon Community College	Schnecksville	PA

Institution	City	State
LIM College	New York	NY
Limestone College	Gaffney	SC
Lindenwood University	Saint Charles	MO
Linn-Benton Community College	Albany	OR
Loyola University Maryland	Baltimore	MD
Macalester College	Saint Paul	MN
Manchester Community College	Manchester	NH
Massachusetts Institute of Technology	Cambridge	MA
McHenry County College	Crystal Lake	IL
McLennan Community College	Waco	TX
McPherson College	McPherson	KS
Miami Dade College	Miami	FL
Minnesota State University-Mankato	Mankato	MN
Missouri State University-West Plains	West Plains	MO
Montclair State University	Montclair	NJ
Moreno Valley College	Moreno Valley	CA
Morningside College	Sioux City	IA
Morrisville State College	Morrisville	NY
Mount Holyoke College	South Hadley	MA
Mountain View College	Dallas	TX
National University College-Bayamon	Bayamon	PR
Norfolk State University	Norfolk	VA
North Carolina Central University	Durham	NC
North Central Missouri College	Trenton	MO
North Dakota State College of Science	Wahpeton	ND
Northeastern Illinois University	Chicago	IL
Northern Illinois University	Dekalb	IL
Northern Oklahoma College	Tonkawa	OK
Ohio State University Agricultural Technical Institute	Wooster	OH
Ohio University-Main Campus	Athens	OH
Ohio Valley University	Vienna	WV
Pace University-New York	New York	NY
Pacific Lutheran University	Tacoma	WA
Palo Alto College	San Antonio	TX
Pasadena City College	Pasadena	CA
Paul Quinn College	Dallas	TX
Pennsylvania State University-Main Campus	University Park	PA
Regis College	Weston	MA
Rhode Island College	Providence	RI
Rich Mountain Community College	Mena	AR
Ringling College of Art and Design	Sarasota	FL
Robert Morris University	Moon Township	PA
Rose-Hulman Institute of Technology	Terre Haute	IN

Institution	City	State
Salisbury University	Salisbury	MD
School of Advertising Art Inc.	Kettering	OH
School of the Art Institute of Chicago	Chicago	IL
Seton Hall University	South Orange	NJ
Shaw University	Raleigh	NC
Sonoma State University	Rohnert Park	CA
South Dakota State University	Brookings	SD
Southeast Missouri State University	Cape Girardeau	MO
Southeastern Community College	Whiteville	NC
St. Catherine University	Saint Paul	MN
SUNY at Albany	Albany	NY
SUNY College of Technology at Alfred	Alfred	NY
Susquehanna University	Selinsgrove	PA
Temple University	Philadelphia	PA
Tennessee Technological University	Cookeville	TN
Texas Southern University	Houston	TX
The College of Saint Scholastica	Duluth	MN
The New School	New York	NY
The University of Alabama	Tuscaloosa	AL
Thomas Nelson Community College	Hampton	VA
Transylvania University	Lexington	KY
Trine University	Angola	IN
Trinity University	San Antonio	TX
Turtle Mountain Community College	Belcourt	ND
Union College	Barbourville	KY
United States Naval Academy	Annapolis	MD
Universidad Pentecostal Mizpa	Rio Piedras	PR
University of Alabama in Huntsville	Huntsville	AL
University of Central Florida *	Orlando	FL
University of Charleston	Charleston	WV
University of Georgia	Athens	GA
University of Hawaii at Manoa	Honolulu	HI
University of Mississippi	University	MS
University of Nebraska-Lincoln	Lincoln	NE
University of New England	Biddeford	ME
University of North Carolina at Chapel Hill	Chapel Hill	NC
University of Northern Iowa *	Cedar Falls	IA
University of Oregon	Eugene	OR
University of Rhode Island	Kingston	RI
University of Richmond	Richmond	VA
University of South Carolina-Beaufort	Bluffton	SC
University of South Carolina-Columbia *	Columbia	SC
University of Southern Mississippi	Hattiesburg	MS

Institution	City	State
University of West Georgia	Carrollton	GA
University of Wisconsin Colleges	Madison	WI
University of Wisconsin-Madison	Madison	WI
University of Wisconsin-Platteville	Platteville	WI
University of Wyoming	Laramie	WY
Ursuline College	Pepper Pike	OH
Virginia Polytechnic Institute and State University	Blacksburg	VA
Virginia Union University	Richmond	VA
Voorhees College	Denmark	SC
Wake Forest University	Winston Salem	NC
Walters State Community College	Morristown	TN
West Los Angeles College	Culver City	CA
Western Kentucky University	Bowling Green	KY
Westminster College	Salt Lake City	UT
Wichita State University	Wichita	KS
Wiley College	Marshall	TX
William Paterson University of New Jersey *	Wayne	NJ

Appendix C: Response Frequencies From the 2014 National Survey of Sophomore-Year Initiatives

Table C.1
Response Frequencies From the 2014 National Survey of Sophomore-Year Initiatives

Survey question/responses	Institution type				Institution control				Number of undergraduates enrolled										Total	
	Two-year		Four-year		Public		Private		Fewer than 1,000		1,001-3,000		3,001-10,000		10,001-20,000		More than 20,000		Total	
	Freq.	%	Freq.	%	Freq.	%	Freq.	%	Freq.	%	Freq.	%	Freq.	%	Freq.	%	Freq.	%	Freq.	%
Q11. Which of the following institutional efforts have included a specific focus on the sophomore year? (Select all that apply.)																				
Accreditation	28	15.7	53	8.8	41	9.7	35	10.5	15	14.0	27	10.4	32	13.9	3	2.6	2	3.3	79	10.2
Institutional assessment	53	29.8	165	27.5	118	28.0	95	28.4	31	29.5	68	26.3	75	32.6	29	25.0	13	21.3	216	28.0
Grant-funded project	20	11.2	51	8.5	44	10.5	25	7.5	8	7.6	23	8.9	21	9.1	9	7.8	9	14.8	70	9.1
Participation in a national survey	17	9.6	97	16.2	57	13.5	55	16.5	11	10.5	36	13.9	42	18.3	16	13.8	8	13.1	113	14.7
Program self-study	29	16.3	94	15.7	158	45.4	41	44.1	20	19.0	29	11.2	46	20.0	18	15.5	8	13.1	121	15.7
Retention study	60	33.7	257	42.8	167	39.7	135	40.4	37	35.2	114	44.0	89	38.7	47	40.5	27	44.3	314	40.7
Strategic planning	37	20.8	164	27.3	102	24.2	89	26.6	20	19.0	75	29.0	65	28.3	26	22.4	13	21.3	199	25.8
Other	10	5.6	39	6.5	28	6.7	20	6.0	4	3.8	15	5.8	18	7.8	8	6.9	4	6.6	49	6.4
Institution is not engaged in any of these	85	47.8	239	39.8	183	43.5	135	40.4	48	45.7	101	39.0	95	41.3	51	44.0	26	42.6	321	41.6
Total	178	100.0	600	100.0	228	100.0	191	100.0	105	100.0	259	100.0	230	100.0	116	100.0	61	100.0	771	100.0
Q12. How long have your institutional efforts included a specific focus on the sophomore year?																				
1 year or less	17	18.7	67	19.5	46	20.2	34	17.8	9	17.0	31	20.1	25	19.1	8	12.9	10	32.3	83	19.3
2-5 years	50	54.9	207	60.2	137	60.1	111	58.1	29	54.7	93	60.4	74	56.5	41	66.1	18	58.1	255	59.2
6-10 years	16	17.6	41	11.9	32	14.0	25	13.1	8	15.1	16	10.4	23	17.6	8	12.9	1	3.2	56	13.0
11-15 years	4	4.4	14	4.1	8	3.5	9	4.7	1	1.9	8	5.2	4	3.1	3	4.8	2	6.5	18	4.2
16-20 years	3	3.3	3	0.9	4	1.8	2	1.0	1	1.9	1	0.6	2	1.5	2	3.2	0	0.0	6	1.4
More than 20 years	1	1.1	12	3.5	1	0.4	10	5.2	5	9.4	5	3.2	3	2.3	0	0.0	0	0.0	13	3.0
Total	91	100.0	344	100.0	228	100.0	191	100.0	53	100.0	154	100.0	131	100.0	62	100.0	31	100.0	431	100.0

Table continues on page 69

Table continued from page 68

Survey question/responses	Institution type				Institution control				Number of undergraduates enrolled										Total	
	Two-year		Four-year		Public		Private		Fewer than 1,000		1,001 - 3,000		3,001 - 10,000		10,001 - 20,000		More than 20,000			
	Freq.	%	Freq.	%	Freq.	%	Freq.	%	Freq.	%	Freq.	%	Freq.	%	Freq.	%	Freq.	%	Freq.	%
Q13. Which of the following campuswide objectives has your institution created specifically for the sophomore year? (Select all that apply.)																				
Academic assistance	41	44.1	158	45.4	104	45.0	83	42.8	29	53.7	58	37.4	66	49.6	25	39.1	18	58.1	196	44.9
Academic skills	27	29.0	113	32.5	72	31.2	59	30.4	18	33.3	49	31.6	47	35.3	17	26.6	8	25.8	139	31.8
Career exploration	44	47.3	192	55.2	118	51.1	110	56.7	26	48.1	88	56.8	73	54.9	31	48.4	17	54.8	235	53.8
Career preparation (e.g., internships, co-ops)	57	61.3	143	41.1	107	46.3	86	44.3	28	51.9	73	47.1	60	45.1	24	37.5	12	38.7	197	45.1
Civic responsibility	24	25.8	85	24.4	58	25.1	46	23.7	16	29.6	35	22.6	34	25.6	15	23.4	7	22.6	107	24.5
Connection with the institution	13	14.0	139	39.9	69	29.9	76	39.2	16	29.6	49	31.6	47	35.3	26	40.6	12	38.7	150	34.3
Critical-thinking skills	30	32.3	73	21.0	59	25.5	36	18.6	15	27.8	29	18.7	40	30.1	10	15.6	7	22.6	101	23.1
Financial literacy	24	25.8	63	18.1	52	22.5	27	13.9	14	25.9	28	18.1	23	17.3	15	23.4	6	19.4	86	19.7
Graduation rates	57	61.3	81	23.3	98	42.4	36	18.6	18	33.3	34	21.9	42	31.6	29	45.3	12	38.7	135	30.9
Information literacy	15	16.1	47	13.5	32	13.9	23	11.9	12	22.2	17	11.0	17	12.8	11	17.2	4	12.9	61	14.0
Institutional resources and information	15	16.1	85	24.4	51	22.1	43	22.2	12	22.2	32	20.6	32	24.1	15	23.4	9	29.0	100	22.9
Intercultural competence	17	18.3	49	14.1	31	13.4	31	16.0	10	18.5	20	12.9	23	17.3	6	9.4	6	19.4	65	14.9
Leadership opportunities	37	39.8	155	44.5	91	39.4	92	47.4	27	50.0	70	45.2	56	42.1	22	34.4	16	51.6	191	43.7
Oral communication skills	24	25.8	57	16.4	42	18.2	31	16.0	15	27.8	26	16.8	26	19.5	9	14.1	3	9.7	79	18.1
Preprofessional preparation (e.g. premed, prelaw)	4	4.3	40	11.5	21	9.1	20	10.3	8	14.8	11	7.1	15	11.3	8	12.5	2	6.5	44	10.1
Retention	57	61.3	217	62.4	151	65.4	110	56.7	31	57.4	90	58.1	82	61.7	45	70.3	23	74.2	271	62.0
Selection of a major	20	21.5	178	51.1	105	45.5	91	46.9	21	38.9	66	42.6	55	41.4	32	50.0	22	71.0	196	44.9

Table continues on page 70

Table continued from page 69

Survey question/responses	Institution type				Institution control				Number of undergraduates enrolled										Total	
	Two-year		Four-year		Public		Private		Fewer than 1,000		1,001–3,000		3,001–10,000		10,001–20,000		More than 20,000			
	Freq.	%	Freq.	%	Freq.	%	Freq.	%	Freq.	%	Freq.	%	Freq.	%	Freq.	%	Freq.	%	Freq.	%
Q13. Which of the following campuswide objectives has your institution created specifically for the sophomore year? (Select all that apply.) *(continued)*																				
Self-exploration or personal development	10	10.8	107	30.7	48	20.8	64	33.0	17	31.5	38	24.5	38	28.6	17	26.6	7	22.6	117	26.8
Service-learning	25	26.9	103	29.6	69	29.9	55	28.4	17	31.5	39	25.2	40	30.1	21	32.8	9	29.0	126	28.8
Student engagement	37	39.8	153	44.0	99	42.9	80	41.2	21	38.9	59	38.1	66	49.6	29	45.3	13	41.9	188	43.0
Student satisfaction	40	43.0	91	26.1	66	28.6	55	28.4	24	44.4	44	28.4	36	27.1	17	26.6	9	29.0	130	29.7
Student-faculty interaction	25	29.6	103	26.9	64	27.7	57	29.4	19	35.2	40	25.8	40	30.1	19	29.7	8	25.8	126	28.8
Study skills	18	19.4	74	21.3	48	20.8	36	18.6	18	33.3	25	16.1	30	22.6	12	18.8	6	19.4	91	20.8
Support network or friendships	9	9.7	70	20.1	33	14.3	41	21.1	12	22.2	29	18.7	21	15.8	8	12.5	8	25.8	78	17.8
Writing skills	16	17.2	77	22.1	46	19.9	38	19.6	19	35.2	26	16.8	29	21.8	10	15.6	7	22.6	91	20.8
Other	12	12.9	39	11.2	30	13.0	21	10.8	6	11.1	16	10.3	14	10.5	9	14.1	5	16.1	50	11.4
Our institution has not yet created campuswide objectives specifically for the sophomore year	5	5.4	35	10.1	20	8.7	20	10.3	3	5.6	16	10.3	17	12.8	4	6.3	0	0.0	40	9.2
Total	93	100.0	348	100.0	231	100.0	194	100.0	54	100.0	155	100.0	133	100.0	64	100.0	31	100.0	437	100.0
Q14. Does your institution currently offer any initiatives specifically or intentionally geared toward sophomore students?																				
Yes	61	35.1	288	49.4	174	42.5	164	50.3	43	42.6	115	45.1	116	51.6	47	42.0	27	0.0	348	47.4
No	104	59.8	271	46.5	212	51.8	153	46.9	56	55.4	135	52.9	96	42.7	58	51.8	25	43.9	370	43.9
I don't know.	9	5.2	24	4.1	23	5.6	9	2.8	2	2.0	5	2.0	13	5.8	7	6.3	5	8.8	32	8.8
Total	174	100.0	583	100.0	409	100.0	326	100.0	101	100.0	255	100.0	225	100.0	112	100.0	57	100.0	750	100.0

Table continues on page 71

Table continued from page 70

Survey question/responses	Institution type				Institution control				Number of undergraduates enrolled										Total	
	Two-year		Four-year		Public		Private		Fewer than 1,000		1,001 - 3,000		3,001 - 10,000		10,001 - 20,000		More than 20,000			
	Freq.	%	Freq.	%	Freq.	%	Freq.	%	Freq.	%	Freq.	%	Freq.	%	Freq.	%	Freq.	%	Freq.	%
Q15. Please indicate the reason(s) why your institution does not have a sophomore initiative: (Select all that apply.)																				
Lack of expertise	12	10.9	36	12.4	25	11.0	21	13.0	10	17.2	21	15.1	11	10.4	4	6.5	1	3.3	47	11.9
Lack of funding	36	32.7	99	34.0	78	34.2	56	34.6	16	27.6	53	38.1	40	37.7	19	30.6	6	20.0	134	33.9
Lack of staff or faculty buy-in	12	10.9	62	21.3	31	13.6	40	24.7	19	32.8	31	22.3	18	17.0	6	9.7	0	0.0	74	18.7
Limited time	36	32.7	106	36.4	78	34.2	58	35.8	16	27.6	60	43.2	42	39.6	17	27.4	6	20.0	141	35.7
Not an institutional priority	34	30.9	108	37.1	70	30.7	68	42.0	25	43.1	55	39.6	35	33.0	19	30.6	6	20.0	140	35.4
Other	50	45.5	118	40.5	103	45.2	61	37.7	23	39.7	51	36.7	38	35.8	34	54.8	7	23.3	163	41.3
Total	110	100.0	291	100.0	228	100.0	162	100.0	58	100.0	139	100.0	106	100.0	62	100.0	30	100.0	395	100.0
Q16. Has your institution had initiatives specifically or intentionally geared toward sophomore students in the past five years?																				
Yes	13	11.9	30	10.3	24	10.6	19	11.7	4	6.9	18	12.9	8	7.6	8	12.9	5	16.7	43	10.9
No	77	70.6	227	78.0	171	75.3	127	78.4	48	82.8	101	72.7	84	80.0	46	74.2	21	70.0	300	76.1
I don't know.	19	17.4	34	11.7	32	14.1	16	9.9	6	10.3	20	14.4	13	12.4	8	12.9	4	13.3	51	12.9
Total	109	100.0	291	100.0	227	100.0	162	100.0	58	100.0	139	100.0	105	100.0	62	100.0	30	100.0	394	100.0
Q17. Please indicate which of the following sophomore initiative(s) your institution had in the past five years: (Select all that apply.)																				
Academic advising	8	61.5	14	50.0	13	56.5	9	50.0	4	100.0	8	44.4	3	42.9	4	50.0	3	75.0	22	53.7
Academic coaching or mentoring	3	23.1	8	28.6	4	17.4	7	38.9	3	75.0	4	22.2	0	0.0	3	37.5	1	25.0	11	26.8
Back-to-school events	3	23.1	6	21.4	5	21.7	4	22.2	4	100.0	1	5.6	1	14.3	2	25.0	1	25.0	9	22.0
Career exploration	7	53.8	9	32.1	10	43.5	6	33.3	2	50.0	6	33.3	4	57.1	3	37.5	1	25.0	16	39.0
Career planning	3	23.1	6	21.4	5	21.7	4	22.2	2	50.0	2	11.1	4	57.1	1	12.5	0	0.0	9	22.0
Class events	3	23.1	3	10.7	3	13.0	3	16.7	2	50.0	2	11.1	1	14.3	0	0.0	1	25.0	6	14.6
Common reading experience	0	0.0	0	0.0	0	0.0	0	0.0	4	100.0	18	100.0	7	100.0	8	100.0	4	100.0	41	100.0

Table continues on page 72

Table continued from page 71

Q17. Please indicate which of the following sophomore initiative(s) your institution had in the past five years: (Select all that apply.) *(continued)*

Survey question/responses	Institution type				Institution control				Number of undergraduates enrolled										Total	
	Two-year		Four-year		Public		Private		Fewer than 1,000		1,001-3,000		3,001-10,000		10,001-20,000		More than 20,000			
	Freq.	%	Freq.	%	Freq.	%	Freq.	%	Freq.	%	Freq.	%	Freq.	%	Freq.	%	Freq.	%	Freq.	%
Course-specific support for classes with high D/F/W rates	3	23.1	4	14.3	6	26.1	1	5.6	1	25.0	0	0.0	1	14.3	3	37.5	2	50.0	7	17.1
Credit-bearing course	2	15.4	0	0.0	2	8.7	0	0.0	0	0.0	1	5.6	0	0.0	1	12.5	0	0.0	2	4.9
Cultural enrichment activities	4	30.8	0	0.0	4	17.4	0	0.0	0	0.0	0	0.0	1	14.3	1	12.5	2	50.0	4	9.8
Early-alert systems	6	46.2	8	28.6	9	39.1	5	27.8	2	50.0	4	22.2	4	57.1	3	37.5	1	25.0	14	34.1
Faculty or staff mentors	1	7.7	4	14.3	1	4.3	4	22.2	1	25.0	3	16.7	0	0.0	0	0.0	1	25.0	5	12.2
Financial aid	3	23.1	1	3.6	3	13.0	1	5.6	1	25.0	0	0.0	2	28.6	1	12.5	0	0.0	4	9.8
Internships	6	46.2	1	3.6	6	26.1	1	5.6	1	25.0	1	5.6	1	14.3	2	25.0	2	50.0	7	17.1
Leadership development	5	38.5	8	28.6	7	30.4	6	33.3	3	75.0	3	16.7	2	28.6	3	37.5	2	50.0	13	31.7
Learning communities	4	30.8	1	3.6	5	21.7	0	0.0	0	0.0	0	0.0	1	14.3	3	37.5	1	25.0	5	12.2
Major exploration and selection	2	15.4	10	35.7	6	26.1	6	33.3	1	25.0	4	22.2	3	42.9	3	37.5	1	25.0	12	29.3
Online communications	1	7.7	2	7.1	2	8.7	1	5.6	1	25.0	0	0.0	0	0.0	2	25.0	0	0.0	3	7.3
Opportunities to coteach	0	0.0	2	7.0	1	4.3	1	5.6	1	25.0	0	0.0	0	0.0	1	12.5	0	0.0	2	4.9
Outdoor or wilderness adventure	0	0.0	1	3.6	1	4.3	0	0.0	0	0.0	0	0.0	1	14.3	0	0.0	0	0.0	1	2.4
Peer mentoring by sophomores	4	30.8	6	21.4	7	30.4	3	16.7	1	25.0	3	16.7	1	14.3	5	62.5	0	0.0	10	24.4
Peer mentors for sophomores	1	7.7	5	17.9	2	8.7	4	22.2	1	25.0	2	11.1	1	14.3	1	12.5	1	25.0	6	14.6
Print publications	0	0.0	0	0.0		0.0	0	0.0	0	0.0	0	0.0	0	0.0	0	0.0	0	0.0	0	0.0
Residence life - sophomore live on-campus requirement	0	0.0	5	17.9	0	0.0	5	27.8	2	50.0	3	16.7	0	0.0	0	0.0	0	0.0	5	12.2

Table continues on page 73

Table continued from page 72

Survey question/responses	Institution type				Institution control				Number of undergraduates enrolled										Total	
	Two-year		Four-year		Public		Private		Fewer than 1,000		1,001 - 3,000		3,001 - 10,000		10,001 - 20,000		More than 20,000			
	Freq.	%	Freq.	%	Freq.	%	Freq.	%	Freq.	%	Freq.	%	Freq.	%	Freq.	%	Freq.	%	Freq.	%
Q17. Please indicate which of the following sophomore initiative(s) your institution had in the past five years: (Select all that apply.) *(continued)*																				
Residence life - sophomore-specific living learning community	0	0.0	0	0.0	0	0.0	0	0.0	0	0.0	0	0.0	0	0.0	0	0.0	0	0.0	0	0.0
Residence life- sophomore-specific residential curriculum	0	0.0	1	3.6	0	0.0	1	5.6	0	0.0	1	5.6	0	0.0	0	0.0	0	0.3	1	2.4
Retreats	0	0.0	1	3.6	0	0.0	1	5.6	1	25.0	0	0.0	0	0.0	0	0.0	0	0.0	1	2.4
Service-learning or community service	6	46.2	3	10.7	8	34.8	1	5.6	1	25.0	2	11.1	1	14.3	2	25.0	3	75.0	9	22.0
Student government	2	15.4	3	10.7	3	13.0	2	11.1	2	50.0	0	0.0	1	14.3	1	12.5	1	25.0	5	12.2
Study abroad	4	30.8	3	10.7	5	21.7	2	11.1	1	25.0	1	5.6	2	28.6	1	12.5	2	50.0	7	17.1
Summer bridge program	1	7.7	1	3.6	1	4.3	1	5.6	1	25.0	1	5.6	0	0.0	0	0.0	0	0.0	2	4.9
Summer newsletter or communication	0	0.0	1	3.6	0	0.0	1	5.6	1	25.0	0	0.0	0	0.0	0	0.0	0	0.0	1	2.4
Undergraduate research	1	7.7	24	14.3	4	17.4	1	5.6	1	25.0	0	0.0	0	0.0	3	37.5	1	25.0	5	12.2
Other	3	23.1	5	17.9	6	26.1	2	11.1	0	0.0	5	27.8	2	28.6	0	0.0	1	25.0	8	19.5
Total	13	100.0	28	100.0	23	100.0	18	100.0	4	100.0	18	100.0	7	100.0	8	100.0	4	100.0	41	100.0
Q18. Is your institution considering or developing any future initiatives specifically or intentionally geared toward sophomore students?																				
Yes	39	36.1	155	54.0	106	46.9	83	52.5	22	38.6	71	51.8	54	51.9	31	50.0	16	55.2	194	49.9
No	43	39.8	87	30.3	73	32.3	54	34.2	32	56.1	37	27.0	34	32.7	17	27.4	8	27.6	128	32.9
I don't know.	26	24.1	45	15.7	47	20.8	21	13.3	3	5.3	29	21.2	16	15.4	14	22.6	5	17.2	67	17.2
Total	108	100.0	287	100.0	226	100.0	158	100.0	57	100.0	137	100.0	104	100.0	62	100.0	29	100.0	389	100.0

Table continues on page 74

Table continued from page 73

| Survey question/responses | Institution type | | | | Institution control | | | | Number of undergraduates enrolled | | | | | | | | | | Total | |
| | Two-year | | Four-year | | Public | | Private | | Fewer than 1,000 | | 1,001 - 3,000 | | 3,001 - 10,000 | | 10,001 - 20,000 | | More than 20,000 | | | |
	Freq.	%	Freq.	%	Freq.	%	Freq.	%	Freq.	%	Freq.	%	Freq.	%	Freq.	%	Freq.	%	Freq.	%
Q19. Please indicate which of the following future sophomore initiative(s) your institution is considering or developing: (Select all that apply.)																				
Academic advising	27	71.1	89	58.2	70	67.3	41	50.0	12	57.1	39	55.7	34	63.0	22	73.3	9	56.3	116	60.7
Academic coaching or mentoring	19	50.0	72	47.1	53	51.0	36	43.9	6	28.6	32	45.7	31	57.4	14	46.7	8	50.0	91	47.6
Back-to-school events	6	15.8	33	21.6	20	19.2	18	22.0	5	23.8	17	24.3	11	20.4	5	16.7	1	6.3	39	20.4
Career exploration	3	7.9	6	40.0	10	52.6	31	60.8	9	42.9	41	58.6	30	55.6	20	66.7	7	43.8	107	56.0
Career planning	20	52.6	78	51.0	55	52.9	40	48.8	8	38.1	38	54.3	31	57.4	16	53.3	5	31.3	98	51.3
Class events	24	63.2	2	1.3	8	7.7	17	20.7	3	14.3	15	21.4	6	11.1	2	6.7	0	0.0	26	13.6
Common reading experience	2	5.3	10	6.5	9	8.7	3	3.7	0	0.0	3	4.3	6	11.1	2	6.7	1	6.3	12	6.3
Course-specific support for classes with high D/F/W rates	12	31.6	34	22.2	38	36.5	8	9.8	2	9.5	8	11.4	17	31.5	13	43.3	6	37.5	46	24.1
Credit-bearing course	3	7.9	8	5.2	7	6.7	4	4.9	1	4.8	5	7.1	3	5.6	1	3.3	1	6.3	11	5.8
Cultural enrichment activities	4	10.5	15	9.8	12	11.5	6	7.3	2	9.5	6	8.6	6	11.1	4	13.3	1	6.3	19	9.9
Early-alert systems	21	55.3	72	47.1	61	58.7	29	35.4	6	28.6	28	40.0	33	61.1	19	63.3	7	43.8	93	48.7
Faculty or staff mentors	9	23.7	32	20.9	22	21.2	7	20.7	4	19.0	14	20.0	15	27.8	5	16.7	3	18.8	41	21.5
Financial aid	5	13.2	14	9.2	11	10.6	6	7.3	1	4.8	9	12.9	5	9.3	2	6.7	2	12.5	19	9.9
Internships	13	34.2	36	23.5	29	27.9	19	23.2	2	9.5	17	24.3	16	29.6	9	30.0	5	31.3	49	25.7
Leadership development	11	28.9	68	44.4	39	37.5	37	45.1	9	42.9	37	52.9	16	29.6	13	43.3	4	25.0	79	41.4
Learning communities	11	28.9	30	19.6	28	26.9	12	14.6	2	9.5	13	18.6	14	25.9	9	30.0	3	18.8	41	21.5
Major exploration and selection	5	13.2	52	34.0	35	33.7	21	25.6	2	9.5	17	24.3	19	35.2	11	36.7	8	50.0	57	29.8
Online communications	2	5.3	18	11.8	12	11.5	8	9.8	1	4.8	6	8.6	8	14.8	3	10.0	2	12.5	20	10.5

Table continues on page 75

Table continued from page 74

Q19. Please indicate which of the following future sophomore initiative(s) your institution is considering or developing: (Select all that apply.) (continued)

Survey question/responses	Institution type				Institution control				Number of undergraduates enrolled										Total	
	Two-year		Four-year		Public		Private		Fewer than 1,000		1,001-3,000		3,001-10,000		10,001-20,000		More than 20,000			
	Freq.	%	Freq.	%	Freq.	%	Freq.	%	Freq.	%	Freq.	%	Freq.	%	Freq.	%	Freq.	%	Freq.	%
Opportunities to coteach	0	0.0	8	5.2	4	3.8	4	4.9	1	4.8	3	4.3	3	5.6	1	3.3	0	0.0	8	4.2
Outdoor or wilderness adventure	0	0.0	4	2.6	2	1.9	2	2.4	0	0.0	1	1.4	3	5.6	0	0.0	0	0.0	4	2.1
Peer mentoring by sophomores	15	39.5	42	27.5	35	33.7	20	24.4	3	14.3	23	32.9	16	29.6	9	30.0	6	37.5	57	29.8
Peer mentors for sophomores	0	0.0	21	13.7	14	13.5	7	8.5	2	9.5	5	7.1	8	14.8	5	16.7	1	6.3	21	11.0
Print publications	0	0.0	2	1.3	0	0.0	2	1.9	0	0.0	0	0.0	1	1.9	1	3.3	0	0.0	2	1.0
Residence life - sophomore live on-campus requirement	0	0.0	8	5.2	2	1.9	5	6.1	2	9.5	2	2.9	3	5.6	1	3.3	0	0.0	8	4.2
Residence life - sophomore-specific living learning community	0	0.0	17	11.1	7	6.7	10	12.2	1	4.8	8	11.4	5	9.3	2	6.7	1	6.3	17	8.9
Residence life- sophomore-specific residential curriculum	0	0.0	6	3.9	1	1.0	5	6.1	1	4.8	4	5.7	1	1.9	0	0.0	0	0.0	6	3.1
Retreats	0	0.0	9	5.9	2	1.9	7	8.5	2	9.5	5	7.1	2	3.7	0	0.0	0	0.0	9	4.7
Service-learning or community service	17	44.7	49	32.0	42	40.4	22	26.8	4	19.0	27	38.6	18	33.3	9	30.0	8	50.0	66	34.6
Student government	4	10.5	5	3.3	5	4.8	2	2.4	3	14.3	3	4.3	2	3.7	0	0.0	1	6.3	9	4.7
Study abroad	7	18.4	25	16.3	22	21.2	8	9.8	3	14.3	9	12.9	10	18.5	7	23.3	3	18.8	32	16.8
Summer bridge program	4	10.5	8	5.2	5	4.8	5	6.1	3	14.3	5	7.1	3	5.6	0	0.0	1	6.3	12	6.3
Summer newsletter or communication	0	0.0	11	7.2	4	3.8	7	8.5	2	9.5	3	4.3	6	11.1	0	0.0	0	0.0	11	5.8
Undergraduate research	3	7.9	37	24.2	31	29.8	8	9.8	4	19.0	9	12.9	13	24.1	7	23.3	7	43.8	40	20.9
Other	4	10.5	15	9.8	10	9.6	9	11.0	4	19.0	5	7.1	3	5.6	5	16.7	2	12.5	19	9.9
Total	38	100.0	153	100.0	104	100.0	82	100.0	21	100.0	70	100.0	54	100.0	30	100.0	16	100.0	191	100.0

Table continues on page 76

Table continued from page 75

Survey question/responses	Institution type				Institution control				Number of undergraduates enrolled										Total	
	Two-year		Four-year		Public		Private		Fewer than 1,000		1,001-3,000		3,001-10,000		10,001-20,000		More than 20,000			
	Freq.	%	Freq.	%	Freq.	%	Freq.	%	Freq.	%	Freq.	%	Freq.	%	Freq.	%	Freq.	%	Freq.	%
Q20. In which of the following areas does your institution currently have initiatives specifically or intentionally geared toward sophomore students? (Select all that apply.)																				
Academic advising	40	66.7	160	55.7	108	62.4	84	51.5	25	59.5	60	52.2	69	60.0	30	63.8	15	55.6	199	57.5
Academic coaching or mentoring	17	28.3	88	30.7	57	32.9	42	25.8	15	35.7	30	26.1	34	29.6	14	29.8	11	40.7	104	30.1
Back-to-school events	10	16.7	71	24.1	37	21.4	43	26.4	9	21.4	28	24.3	29	25.2	8	17.0	7	25.9	81	23.4
Career exploration	26	43.3	157	54.7	86	49.7	94	57.7	23	54.8	68	59.1	55	47.8	23	48.9	14	51.9	183	52.9
Career planning	29	48.3	140	48.8	78	45.1	86	52.8	22	52.4	59	51.3	58	50.4	21	44.7	9	33.3	169	48.8
Class events	15	25.0	83	28.9	30	17.3	63	38.7	17	40.5	39	33.9	28	24.3	11	23.4	3	11.1	98	28.3
Common reading experience	4	6.7	16	5.6	9	5.2	5	5.5	6	14.3	4	3.5	7	6.1	2	4.3	1	3.7	20	5.8
Course-specific support for classes with high D/F/W rates	9	15.0	45	15.7	28	16.2	22	13.5	10	23.8	13	11.3	20	17.4	6	12.8	5	18.5	54	15.6
Credit-bearing course	6	10.0	36	12.5	17	9.8	23	14.1	11	26.2	10	8.7	14	12.2	3	6.4	4	14.8	42	12.1
Cultural enrichment activities	10	16.7	49	17.1	27	15.6	31	19.0	11	26.2	18	15.7	23	20.0	6	12.8	1	3.7	59	17.1
Early-alert systems	28	46.7	120	41.8	73	42.2	71	43.6	17	40.5	55	47.8	51	44.3	18	38.3	6	22.2	147	42.5
Faculty or staff mentors	12	20.0	67	23.3	36	20.8	38	23.3	12	28.6	23	20.0	25	21.7	11	23.4	8	29.6	79	22.8
Financial aid	20	33.3	31	10.8	28	16.2	18	11.0	14	33.3	16	13.9	14	12.2	5	10.6	2	7.4	51	14.7
Internships	34	56.7	60	20.9	55	31.8	35	21.5	19	45.2	35	30.4	28	24.3	9	19.1	2	7.4	93	26.9
Leadership development	23	38.2	117	41.1	59	34.1	78	47.9	21	50.0	55	47.8	40	34.8	17	36.2	7	25.9	140	40.5
Online communications	9	15.0	60	20.9	34	19.7	30	18.4	13	31.0	16	13.9	22	19.1	10	21.3	7	25.9	68	19.7
Opportunities to coteach	5	8.3	29	10.1	16	9.2	17	10.4	7	16.7	10	8.7	12	10.4	4	8.5	1	3.7	34	9.8
Outdoor or wilderness adventure	3	5.0	12	4.2	7	4.0	7	4.3	2	4.8	5	4.3	5	4.3	3	6.4	0	0.0	15	4.3
Peer mentoring by sophomores	18	30.0	83	28.9	55	31.8	45	27.6	14	33.3	27	23.5	38	33.0	14	29.8	7	25.9	100	28.9

Table continues on page 77

Table continued from page 76

Q20. In which of the following areas does your institution currently have initiatives specifically or intentionally geared toward sophomore students? (Select all that apply.) *(continued)*

Survey question/responses	Institution type				Institution control				Number of undergraduates enrolled										Total	
	Two-year		Four-year		Public		Private		Fewer than 1,000		1,001 - 3,000		3,001 - 10,000		10,001 - 20,000		More than 20,000			
	Freq.	%	Freq.	%	Freq.	%	Freq.	%	Freq.	%	Freq.	%	Freq.	%	Freq.	%	Freq.	%	Freq.	%
Peer mentors for sophomores	3	5.0	40	13.9	21	12.1	22	13.5	9	21.4	10	8.7	15	13.0	8	17.0	1	3.7	43	12.4
Print publications	1	1.7	21	7.3	13	7.5	9	5.5	2	4.8	4	3.5	10	8.7	3	6.4	3	11.1	22	6.4
Residence life - sophomore live on-campus requirement	2	3.3	72	25.1	21	12.1	53	32.5	10	23.8	29	25.2	30	26.1	4	8.5	1	3.7	74	21.4
Residence life - sophomore-specific living learning community	1	1.7	56	19.5	27	15.6	30	18.4	1	2.4	16	13.9	22	19.1	10	21.3	8	29.6	57	16.5
Residence life- sophomore-specific residential curriculum	1	1.7	24	8.4	8	4.6	17	10.4	0	0.0	8	7.0	12	10.4	3	6.4	2	7.4	25	7.2
Retreats	3	5.0	27	9.4	6	3.5	24	14.7	6	14.3	11	9.6	12	10.4	1	2.1	0	0.0	30	8.7
Service-learning or community service	19	31.7	73	25.4	46	26.6	44	27.0	11	26.2	31	27.0	34	29.6	11	23.4	4	14.8	91	26.3
Student government	8	13.3	60	20.9	23	13.3	43	26.4	8	19.0	30	26.1	23	20.0	6	12.8	1	3.7	68	19.7
Study abroad	9	15.0	69	24.0	36	20.8	41	25.2	9	21.4	24	20.9	29	25.2	11	23.4	5	18.5	78	22.5
Summer bridge program	5	8.3	8	2.8	8	4.6	5	3.1	3	7.1	3	2.6	5	4.3	2	4.3	0	0.0	13	3.8
Summer newsletter or communication	1	1.7	19	6.6	10	5.8	10	6.1	4	9.5	4	3.5	4	3.5	5	10.6	3	11.1	20	5.8
Undergraduate research	7	11.7	58	20.2	37	21.4	28	17.2	6	14.3	14	12.2	25	21.7	15	31.9	5	18.5	55	15.9
Other	5	8.3	31	10.8	16	9.2	19	11.7	4	9.5	15	13.0	13	11.3	4	8.5	0	0.0	36	10.4
Total	60	100.0	287	100.0	173	100.0	163	100.0	42	100.0	115	100.0	115	100.0	47	100.0	27	100.0	346	100.0

Table continues on page 78

Table continued from page 77

Survey question/responses	Institution type				Institution control				Number of undergraduates enrolled										Total	
	Two-year		Four-year		Public		Private		Fewer than 1,000		1,001 - 3,000		3,001 - 10,000		10,001 - 20,000		More than 20,000			
	Freq.	%	Freq.	%	Freq.	%	Freq.	%	Freq.	%	Freq.	%	Freq.	%	Freq.	%	Freq.	%	Freq.	%
Q21. On your campus, how coordinated are sophomore-year initiatives? (Select the most appropriate answer.)																				
Unknown	0	0.0	3	1.1	1	0.6	2	1.2	1	2.4	1	0.9	0	0.0	0	0.0	1	3.7	3	0.9
1 - Totally decentralized	6	10.2	37	13.0	25	14.5	17	10.6	3	7.1	9	8.0	16	14.0	8	17.0	7	25.9	43	12.5
2	24	40.7	64	22.5	59	34.3	28	17.4	8	19.0	25	22.1	29	25.4	19	40.4	6	22.2	87	25.4
3	21	35.6	101	35.4	55	32.0	62	38.5	16	38.1	48	42.5	40	35.1	11	23.4	7	25.9	122	35.6
4	7	11.9	59	20.7	26	15.1	38	23.6	8	19.0	24	21.2	22	19.3	6	12.8	6	22.2	66	19.2
5 - Totally centralized	1	1.7	21	7.4	6	3.5	14	8.7	6	14.3	6	5.3	7	6.1	3	6.4	0	0.0	22	6.4
Total	59	100.0	285	100.0	172	100.0	161	100.0	42	100.0	113	100.0	114	100.0	47	100.0	27	100.0	343	100.0
Q23. Is there currently an individual in charge of sophomore student programs or initiatives?																				
Yes	8	13.8	106	37.2	47	27.3	64	39.8	14	33.3	46	40.7	33	28.9	12	25.5	9	33.3	114	33.2
No	50	84.7	176	61.8	124	72.1	95	59.0	28	66.7	65	57.5	79	69.3	35	74.5	18	66.7	225	65.6
I don't know.	1	1.7	3	1.1	1	0.6	2	1.2	0	0.0	2	1.8	2	1.8	0	0.0	0	0.0	4	1.2
Total	59	100.0	285	100.0	172	100.0	161	100.0	42	100.0	113	100.0	114	100.0	47	100.0	27	100.0	343	100.0
Q25. Is this position dedicated to sophomore programs and initiatives on a full-time basis (approximately 40 hours per week)?																				
Yes	0	0.0	31	29.8	13	28.3	18	28.1	3	21.4	10	22.2	11	34.4	5	41.7	2	22.2	31	27.7
No	8	100.0	73	70.2	33	71.7	46	71.9	11	78.6	35	77.8	21	65.6	7	58.3	7	77.8	81	72.3
I don't know.	0	0.0	0	0.0	0	0.0	0	0.0	0	0.0	0	0.0	0	0.0	0	0.0	0	0.0	0	0.0
Total	8	100.0	104	100.0	46	100.0	64	100.0	14	100.0	45	100.0	32	100.0	12	100.0	9	100.0	112	100.0
Q26. Does this person have another position on campus?																				
Yes	6	75.0	53	72.6	22	66.7	37	80.4	6	54.5	29	82.9	19	90.5	3	42.9	2	28.6	59	72.8
No	2	25.0	19	26.0	10	30.3	9	19.6	5	45.5	6	17.1	2	9.5	4	57.1	4	57.1	21	25.9
I don't know.	0	0.0	1	1.4	1	3.0	0	0.0	0	0.0	0	0.0	0	0.0	0	0.0	1	14.3	1	1.2
Total	8	100.0	73	100.0	33	100.0	46	100.0	11	100.0	35	100.0	21	100.0	7	100.0	7	100.0	81	100.0

Table continues on page 79

Table continued from page 78

Survey question/responses	Institution type				Institution control				Number of undergraduates enrolled										Total	
	Two-year		Four-year		Public		Private		Fewer than 1,000		1,001-3,000		3,001-10,000		10,001-20,000		More than 20,000			
	Freq.	%	Freq.	%	Freq.	%	Freq.	%	Freq.	%	Freq.	%	Freq.	%	Freq.	%	Freq.	%	Freq.	%
Q27. The other campus role of the dean, director, or coordinator of the sophomore initiative is as a/an: (Select all that apply.)																				
Academic affairs administrator	0	0.0	23	43.4	9	40.9	14	37.8	1	16.7	9	31.0	10	52.6	2	66.7	1	50.0	23	39.0
Faculty member	1	16.7	8	15.1	4	18.2	5	13.5	0	0.0	6	20.7	2	10.5	1	33.3	0	0.0	9	15.3
Student affairs administrator	5	83.3	24	45.3	9	40.9	20	54.1	4	66.7	17	58.6	7	36.8	0	0.0	1	50.0	29	49.2
Other	0	0.0	9	17.0	3	13.6	6	16.2	1	16.7	4	13.8	3	15.8	1	33.3	0	0.0	9	15.3
Total	6	100.0	53	100.0	22	100.0	37	100.0	6	100.0	29	100.0	19	100.0	3	100.0	2	100.0	59	100.0
Q28. Which of the following initiatives reaches the highest proportion of sophomore students at your institution? (Select only one.)																				
Academic advising	27	45.8	129	45.7	89	52.4	63	39.1	16	38.1	44	39.3	52	46.0	29	63.0	14	51.9	155	45.6
Academic coaching or mentoring	2	3.4	9	3.2	4	2.4	6	3.7	4	9.5	2	1.8	5	4.4	0	0.0	0	0.0	11	3.2
Back-to-school events	0	0.0	5	1.8	3	1.8	2	1.2	1	2.4	1	0.9	2	1.8	0	0.0	1	3.7	5	1.5
Career exploration	2	3.4	6	2.1	3	1.8	4	2.5	2	4.8	4	3.6	1	0.9	1	2.2	0	0.0	8	2.4
Career planning	2	3.4	3	1.1	4	2.4	1	0.6	1	2.4	0	0.0	2	1.8	1	2.2	1	3.7	5	1.5
Class events	0	0.0	10	3.5	4	2.4	6	3.7	1	2.4	3	2.7	3	2.7	1	2.2	2	7.4	10	2.9
Common reading experience	0	0.0	1	0.4	0	0.0	1	0.6	1	2.4	0	0.0	0	0.0	0	0.0	0	0.0	1	0.3
Course-specific support for classes with high D/F/W rates	0	0.0	2	0.7	1	0.6	0	0.0	1	2.4	0	0.0	1	0.9	0	0.0	0	0.0	2	0.6
Credit-bearing course	2	3.4	11	3.9	6	3.5	7	4.3	3	7.1	5	4.5	4	3.5	1	2.2	0	0.0	13	3.8
Cultural enrichment activities	1	1.7	2	0.7	2	1.2	1	0.6	0	0.0	2	1.8	1	0.9	0	0.0	0	0.0	3	0.9
Early-alert systems	7	11.9	9	3.2	10	5.9	5	3.1	1	2.4	5	4.5	7	6.2	3	6.5	0	0.0	16	4.7

Table continues on page 80

Table continued from page 79

Survey question/responses	Institution type				Institution control				Number of undergraduates enrolled										Total	
	Two-year		Four-year		Public		Private		Fewer than 1,000		1,001-3,000		3,001-10,000		10,001-20,000		More than 20,000			
	Freq.	%	Freq.	%	Freq.	%	Freq.	%	Freq.	%	Freq.	%	Freq.	%	Freq.	%	Freq.	%	Freq.	%
Q28. Which of the following initiatives reaches the highest proportion of sophomore students at your institution? (Select only one.) *(continued)*																				
Faculty or staff mentors	2	3.4	2	0.7	2	1.2	2	1.2	0	0.0	2	1.8	2	1.8	0	0.0	0	0.0	4	1.2
Financial aid	2	3.4	0	0.0	2	1.2	0	0.0	0	0.0	0	0.0	1	0.9	0	0.0	1	3.7	2	0.6
Internships	5	8.5	1	0.4	5	2.9	1	0.6	3	7.1	2	1.8	1	0.9	0	0.0	0	0.0	6	1.8
Leadership development	0	0.0	5	1.8	0	0.0	5	3.1	0	0.0	4	3.6	1	0.9	0	0.0	0	0.0	5	1.5
Learning communities	0	0.0	1	0.4	0	0.0	1	0.6	0	0.0	1	0.9	0	0.0	0	0.0	0	0.0	1	0.3
Major exploration and selection	0	0.0	7	2.5	2	1.2	5	3.1	2	4.8	4	3.6	1	0.9	0	0.0	0	0.0	7	2.1
Online communications	0	0.0	5	1.2	4	2.4	1	0.6	1	2.4	1	0.9	0	0.0	1	2.2	2	7.4	5	1.5
Opportunities to coteach	0	0.0	0	0.0	0	0.0	0	0.0	0	0.0	0	0.0	0	0.0	0	0.0	0	0.0	0	0.0
Outdoor or wilderness adventure	0	0.0	0	0.0	0	0.0	0	0.0	0	0.0	0	0.0	0	0.0	0	0.0	0	0.0	0	0.0
Peer mentoring by sophomores	0	0.0	2	0.7	1	0.6	1	0.6	0	0.0	1	0.9	1	0.9	0	0.0	0	0.0	2	0.6
Peer mentors for sophomores	0	0.0	0	0.0	0	0.0	0	0.0	0	0.0	0	0.0	0	0.0	0	0.0	0	0.0	0	0.0
Print publications	0	0.0	1	0.4	1	0.6	0	0.0	0	0.0	0	0.0	1	0.9	0	0.0	0	0.0	1	0.3
Residence life - sophomore live on-campus requirement	1	1.7	27	9.6	7	4.1	21	13.0	1	2.4	12	10.7	14	12.4	1	2.2	0	0.0	28	8.2
Residence life - sophomore-specific living-learning community	0	0.0	10	3.5	4	2.4	6	3.7	0	0.0	3	2.7	2	1.8	4	8.7	1	3.7	10	2.9
Residence life - sophomore-specific residential curriculum	0	0.0	4	1.4	2	1.2	2	1.2	0	0.0	1	0.9	2	1.8	1	2.2	0	0.0	4	1.2
Retreats	0	0.0	3	1.1	0	0.0	3	1.9	0	0.0	2	1.8	1	0.9	0	0.0	0	0.0	3	0.9
Service-learning or community service	2	3.4	5	1.8	3	1.8	4	2.5	0	0.0	5	4.5	2	1.8	0	0.0	0	0.0	7	2.1
Student government	2	3.4	2	0.7	2	1.2	1	0.6	2	4.8	0	0.0	2	1.8	0	0.0	0	0.0	4	1.2

Table continues on page 81

Table continued from page 80

Survey question/responses	Institution type				Institution control				Number of undergraduates enrolled										Total	
	Two-year		Four-year		Public		Private		Fewer than 1,000		1,001 - 3,000		3,001 - 10,000		10,001 - 20,000		More than 20,000			
	Freq.	%	Freq.	%	Freq.	%	Freq.	%	Freq.	%	Freq.	%	Freq.	%	Freq.	%	Freq.	%	Freq.	%
Q28. Which of the following initiatives reaches the highest proportion of sophomore students at your institution? (Select only one.) *(continued)*																				
Study abroad	0	0.0	2	0.7	0	0.0	2	1.2	0	0.0	1	0.9	1	0.9	0	0.0	0	0.0	2	0.6
Summer bridge program	0	0.0	0	0.0	0	0.0	0	0.0	0	0.0	0	0.0	0	0.0	0	0.0	0	0.0	0	0.0
Summer newsletter or communication	0	0.0	1	0.4	0	0.0	1	0.6	0	0.0	1	0.9	0	0.0	0	0.0	0	0.0	1	0.3
Undergraduate research	1	1.7	4	1.4	3	1.8	2	1.2	1	2.4	2	1.8	0	0.0	1	2.2	1	3.7	5	1.5
Other	1	1.7	13	4.6	6	3.5	7	4.3	1	2.4	4	3.6	3	2.7	2	4.3	4	14.8	14	4.1
Total	59	100.0	282	100.0	170	100.0	161	100.0	42	100.0	112	100.0	113	100.0	46	100.0	27	100.0	340	100.0
Q29. What is the approximate percentage of sophomore students this initiative reaches on your campus?																				
Less than 10%	5	8.5	20	7.1	19	11.2	6	3.8	0	0.0	7	6.3	11	9.7	3	6.7	4	14.8	25	7.4
10-19%	2	3.4	18	6.4	14	8.3	6	3.8	1	2.4	6	5.4	8	7.1	2	4.4	3	11.1	20	5.9
20-29%	4	6.8	18	6.4	13	7.7	8	5.0	1	2.4	5	4.5	6	5.3	5	11.1	5	18.5	22	6.5
30-39%	8	13.6	13	4.6	13	7.7	8	5.0	1	2.4	9	8.1	6	5.3	2	4.4	3	11.1	21	6.2
40-49%	4	6.8	13	4.6	11	6.5	6	3.8	0	0.0	6	5.4	7	6.2	4	8.9	0	0.0	17	5.0
50-59%	7	11.9	17	6.1	12	7.1	11	6.9	5	11.9	9	8.1	6	5.3	3	6.7	0	0.0	23	6.8
60-69%	4	6.8	17	6.1	15	8.9	6	3.8	1	2.4	3	2.7	8	7.1	6	13.3	3	11.1	21	6.2
70-79%	5	8.5	17	6.1	8	4.7	12	7.5	5	11.9	8	7.2	6	5.3	3	6.7	0	0.0	22	6.5
80-89%	8	13.6	34	12.1	27	16.0	15	9.4	4	9.5	11	9.9	19	16.8	7	15.6	1	3.7	42	12.4
90-99%	6	10.2	57	20.4	20	11.8	39	24.4	8	19.0	24	21.6	20	17.7	6	13.3	5	18.5	63	18.6
100%	6	10.2	56	20.0	17	10.1	45	26.9	16	38.1	23	20.7	16	14.2	4	8.9	3	11.1	62	18.3
Total	59	100.0	280	100.0	169	100.0	160	100.0	42	100.0	111	100.0	113	100.0	45	100.0	27	100.0	338	100.0

Table continues on page 82

Table continued from page 81

Survey question/responses	Institution type				Institution control				Number of undergraduates enrolled										Total	
	Two-year		Four-year		Public		Private		Fewer than 1,000		1,001 - 3,000		3,001 - 10,000		10,001 - 20,000		More than 20,000			
	Freq.	%	Freq.	%	Freq.	%	Freq.	%	Freq.	%	Freq.	%	Freq.	%	Freq.	%	Freq.	%	Freq.	%
Q30. What proportion of your second-year students are required to participate in this initiative? *(continued)*																				
None are required to participate	19	32.2	99	35.2	64	37.6	50	31.3	10	23.8	36	32.4	38	33.6	18	40.0	16	57.1	118	34.8
Less than 10%	4	6.8	11	3.9	12	7.1	2	1.3	1	2.4	4	3.6	4	3.5	4	8.9	1	3.6	14	4.1
10-19%	1	1.7	3	1.1	2	1.2	2	1.3	0	0.0	2	1.8	1	0.9	1	2.2	0	0.0	4	1.2
20-29%	4	6.8	3	1.1	7	4.1	0	0.0	0	0.0	2	1.8	3	2.7	0	0.0	2	7.1	7	2.1
30-39%	3	5.1	1	0.4	4	2.4	0	0.0	0	0.0	0	0.0	3	2.7	1	2.2	0	0.0	4	1.2
40-49%	2	3.4	5	1.8	6	3.5	1	0.6	0	0.0	1	0.9	4	3.5	2	4.4	0	0.0	7	2.1
50-59%	2	3.4	3	1.1	3	1.8	2	1.3	2	4.8	0	0.0	2	1.8	0	0.0	1	3.6	5	1.5
60-69%	1	1.7	6	2.1	4	2.4	3	1.9	2	4.8	1	0.9	2	1.8	2	4.4	0	0.0	7	2.1
70-79%	2	3.4	6	2.1	5	2.9	3	1.9	1	2.4	3	2.7	2	1.8	2	4.4	0	0.0	8	2.4
80-89%	5	8.5	11	3.9	10	5.9	6	3.8	1	2.4	6	5.4	7	6.2	2	4.4	0	0.0	16	4.7
90-99%	1	1.7	11	3.9	3	1.8	8	5.0	1	2.4	4	3.6	5	4.4	1	2.2	1	3.6	12	3.5
100%	15	25.4	122	43.4	50	29.4	83	51.9	24	57.1	52	46.8	42	37.2	12	26.7	7	25.0	137	40.4
Total	59	100.0	281	100.0	170	100.0	160	100.0	42	100.0	111	100.0	113	100.0	45	100.0	28	100.0	339	100.0
Q31. Which of the following groups of second-year students are required to participate in this initiative? (Select all that apply.)																				
Academically underprepared students	7	29.2	20	33.3	19	34.5	8	29.6	0	0.0	9	39.1	11	33.3	4	28.6	3	60.0	27	32.5
First-generation students	4	16.7	11	18.3	10	18.2	5	18.2	1	12.5	4	17.4	6	18.2	3	21.4	1	20.0	15	18.1
Honors students	3	12.5	19	31.7	16	29.1	6	22.2	1	12.5	6	26.1	9	27.3	5	35.7	1	20.0	22	26.5
International students	2	8.3	12	20.0	8	14.5	6	22.2	0	0.0	5	21.7	5	15.2	3	21.4	1	20.0	14	16.9
Learning community participants	3	12.5	13	21.7	12	21.8	4	14.8	0	0.0	2	8.7	9	27.3	4	28.6	1	20.0	16	19.3
Preprofessional students (e.g., prelaw, premed)	0	0.0	13	21.7	9	16.4	4	14.8	0	0.0	4	17.4	5	15.2	2	14.3	2	40.0	13	15.7
Student athletes	3	12.5	18	30.0	5	27.3	6	22.2	0	0.0	5	21.7	9	27.3	4	28.6	3	60.0	21	25.3

Table continues on page 83

Table continued from page 82

Survey question/responses	Institution type				Institution control				Number of undergraduates enrolled										Total	
	Two-year		Four-year		Public		Private		Fewer than 1,000		1,001 - 3,000		3,001 - 10,000		10,001 - 20,000		More than 20,000			
	Freq.	%	Freq.	%	Freq.	%	Freq.	%	Freq.	%	Freq.	%	Freq.	%	Freq.	%	Freq.	%	Freq.	%
Q31. Which of the following groups of second-year students are required to participate in this initiative? (Select all that apply.) *(continued)*																				
Students enrolled in developmental or remedial courses	5	20.8	12	20.0	13	23.6	4	14.8	0	0.0	4	17.4	8	24.2	5	35.7	0	0.0	17	20.5
Students on probationary status	9	37.5	26	43.3	26	47.3	8	29.6	1	12.5	9	39.1	15	45.5	8	57.1	2	40.0	35	42.2
Students participating in dual-enrollment programs	0	0.0	5	8.3	4	7.3	1	3.7	0	0.0	0	0.0	3	9.1	2	14.3	0	0.0	5	6.0
Students residing within a particular residence hall	1	4.2	11	18.3	5	9.1	7	25.9	0	0.0	7	30.4	3	9.1	2	14.3	0	0.0	12	14.5
Students with fewer credits than necessary for sophomore status	1	4.2	12	20.0	6	10.9	7	25.9	0	0.0	5	21.7	5	15.2	2	14.3	1	20.0	13	15.7
Students within specific majors	7	29.2	8	13.3	11	20.0	4	14.8	2	25.0	5	21.7	4	12.1	2	14.3	1	20.0	14	16.9
TRIO participants	3	12.5	12	20.0	12	21.8	3	11.1	1	12.5	2	8.7	8	24.2	3	21.4	1	20.0	15	18.1
Undeclared students	4	16.7	20	33.3	18	32.7	6	22.2	0	0.0	5	21.7	10	30.3	6	42.9	3	60.0	24	28.9
Other	8	33.3	20	33.3.	14	25.5	13	48.1	5	62.5	6	26.1	11	33.3	5	35.7	0	0.0	27	32.5
Total	24	100.0	60	100.0	55	100.0	27	100.0	8	100.0	23	100.0	33	100.0	14	100.0	5	100.0	83	100.0
Q32. Which of the following groups of sophomore students are specifically targeted by this initiative? (Select all that apply.)																				
Academically underprepared students	12	27.9	35	22.0	31	26.1	14	18.2	2	11.1	21	35.6	26	36.6	10	31.3	7	33.3	66	32.8
First-generation students	12	27.9	35	22.0	31	26.1	14	18.2	4	22.2	15	25.4	13	18.3	8	25.0	7	33.3	47	23.4
Honors students	2	4.7	37	23.3	26	21.8	12	15.6	1	5.6	13	22.0	11	15.5	7	21.9	7	33.3	39	19.4
International students	4	9.3	16	10.1	11	9.2	8	10.4	2	11.1	7	11.9	6	8.5	4	12.5	1	4.8	20	10.0
Learning community participants	3	7.0	23	14.0	20	16.8	5	6.5	1	5.6	4	6.8	9	12.7	6	18.8	6	28.6	26	12.9
Preprofessional students (e.g., prelaw, premed)	4	9.3	17	10.7	15	12.6	5	6.5	1	5.6	5	8.5	7	9.9	7	21.9	1	4.8	21	10.4
Student athletes	8	18.6	35	22.0	27	22.7	16	20.8	1	5.6	14	23.7	17	23.9	7	21.9	4	19.0	43	21.4

Table continues on page 84

Table continued from page 83

Survey question/responses	Institution type				Institution control				Number of undergraduates enrolled										Total	
	Two-year		Four-year		Public		Private		Fewer than 1,000		1,001 - 3,000		3,001 - 10,000		10,001 - 20,000		More than 20,000			
	Freq.	%	Freq.	%	Freq.	%	Freq.	%	Freq.	%	Freq.	%	Freq.	%	Freq.	%	Freq.	%	Freq.	%
Q32. Which of the following groups of sophomore students are specifically targeted by this initiative? (Select all that apply.) *(continued)*																				
Students enrolled in developmental or remedial courses	10	23.3	17	10.7	20	16.8	7	9.1	1	5.6	8	13.6	11	15.5	6	18.8	1	4.8	27	13.4
Students on probationary status	17	39.5	49	30.8	44	37.0	19	24.7	2	11.1	20	33.9	29	40.8	9	28.1	5	23.8	65	32.3
Students participating in dual-enrollment programs	3	7.0	1	0.6	4	3.4	0	0.0	0	0.0	0	0.0	3	4.2	0	0.0	0	0.0	3	1.5
Students residing within a particular residence hall	3	7.0	24	15.1	14	11.8	13	16.9	0	0.0	11	18.6	9	12.7	3	9.4	4	19.0	27	13.4
Students with fewer credits than necessary for sophomore status	3	7.0	15	9.4	14	11.8	4	5.2	0	0.0	4	6.8	6	8.5	3	9.4	5	23.8	18	9.0
Students within specific majors	7	16.3	13	8.2	16	13.4	4	5.2	4	22.2	4	6.8	4	5.6	5	15.6	2	9.5	19	9.5
TRIO participants	7	16.3	17	10.7	20	16.8	4	5.2	1	5.6	5	8.5	10	14.1	5	15.6	3	14.3	24	11.9
Undeclared students	8	18.6	44	27.7	35	29.4	17	21.1	2	11.1	14	23.7	20	28.2	8	25.0	8	38.1	52	25.9
Other	15	34.9	64	40.3	43	36.1	34	44.2	10	55.6	17	28.8	31	43.7	13	40.6	7	33.3	78	38.8
Total	43	100.0	159	100.0	119	100.0	77	100.0	18	100.0	59	100.0	71	100.0	32	100.0	21	100.0	201	100.0
Q33. How long has this initiative been in place?																				
2 years or less	14	24.1	73	26.4	48	28.9	36	22.6	6	14.3	35	31.5	22	19.8	14	31.8	10	38.5	87	26.0
3-5 years	11	19.0	66	23.8	42	25.3	31	19.5	9	21.4	21	18.9	24	21.6	16	36.4	7	26.9	77	23.1
6-10 years	15	25.9	47	17.0	34	20.5	27	17.0	8	19.0	19	17.1	26	23.4	5	11.4	4	15.4	62	18.6
11-15 years	3	5.2	20	7.2	10	6.0	13	8.2	2	4.8	7	6.3	9	8.1	2	4.5	2	7.7	22	6.6
16-20 years	3	5.2	11	4.0	6	3.6	8	5.0	3	7.1	3	2.7	6	5.4	1	2.3	1	3.8	14	4.2
More than 20 years	12	20.7	60	21.7	26	15.7	44	27.7	14	33.3	26	23.4	24	21.6	6	13.6	2	7.7	72	21.6
Total	58	100.0	277	100.0	166	100.0	159	100.0	42	100.0	111	100.0	111	100.0	44	100.0	26	100.0	334	100.0

Table continues on page 85

Table continued from page 84

Q34. Please select the three most important objectives for this initiative:

Survey question/responses	Institution type				Institution control				Number of undergraduates enrolled										Total	
	Two-year		Four-year		Public		Private		Fewer than 1,000		1,001 - 3,000		3,001 - 10,000		10,001 - 20,000		More than 20,000		Total	
	Freq.	%	Freq.	%	Freq.	%	Freq.	%	Freq.	%	Freq.	%	Freq.	%	Freq.	%	Freq.	%	Freq.	%
Academic assistance	30	51.7	112	40.4	80	48.2	57	35.8	14	33.3	43	38.7	54	48.6	22	50.0	9	34.6	142	42.5
Academic skills	10	17.2	33	11.9	25	15.1	17	10.7	8	19.0	14	12.6	13	11.7	7	15.9	1	3.8	43	12.9
Career exploration	9	15.5	48	17.3	29	17.5	27	17.0	5	11.9	24	21.6	14	12.6	10	22.7	4	15.4	57	17.1
Career preparation (e.g., internships, co-ops)	15	25.9	25	9.0	26	15.7	12	7.5	9	21.4	8	7.2	13	11.7	5	11.4	4	15.4	39	11.7
Civic responsibility	3	5.2	14	5.1	6	3.6	10	6.3	3	7.1	6	5.4	7	6.3	0	0.0	1	3.8	17	5.1
Connection with the institution	10	17.2	70	25.3	34	20.5	44	27.7	8	19.0	27	24.3	29	26.1	9	20.5	7	26.9	80	24.0
Critical-thinking skills	3	5.2	15	5.4	8	4.8	10	6.3	3	7.1	6	5.4	6	5.4	2	4.5	1	3.8	18	5.4
Financial literacy	2	3.4	3	1.1	3	1.8	0	0.0	1	2.4	0	0.0	4	3.6	0	0.0	0	0.0	5	1.5
Graduation rates	22	37.9	44	15.9	48	28.9	17	10.7	10	23.8	14	12.6	22	19.8	12	27.3	7	26.9	65	19.5
Information literacy	2	3.4	3	1.1	3	1.8	1	0.6	3	7.1	0	0.0	2	1.8	0	0.0	0	0.0	5	1.5
Institutional resources and information	2	3.4	37	13.4	20	12.0	17	10.7	4	9.5	10	9.0	12	10.8	6	13.6	7	26.9	39	11.7
Intercultural competence	2	3.4	8	2.9	4	2.4	6	3.8	1	2.4	5	4.5	3	2.7	0	0.0	1	3.8	10	3.0
Leadership opportunities	4	6.9	18	6.5	11	6.6	11	6.9	2	4.8	9	8.1	7	6.3	3	6.8	1	3.8	22	6.6
Oral communication skills	0	0.0	2	0.7	0	0.0	2	1.3	0	0.0	2	1.8	0	0.0	0	0.0	0	0.0	2	0.6
Preprofessional preparation (e.g. premed, prelaw)	2	3.4	4	1.4	1	0.6	3	1.9	3	7.1	3	2.7	0	0.0	0	0.0	0	0.0	6	1.8
Retention	25	43.1	117	42.2	83	50.0	53	33.3	13	31.0	40	36.0	54	48.6	21	47.7	13	50.0	141	42.2
Selection of a major	5	8.6	58	20.9	31	18.7	32	20.1	9	21.4	22	19.8	13	11.7	13	29.5	6	23.1	63	18.9
Self-exploration or personal development	3	5.2	53	19.1	15	9.0	41	25.8	8	19.0	26	23.4	17	15.3	2	4.5	3	11.5	56	16.8
Student engagement	5	8.6	68	24.5	24	14.5	48	30.2	9	21.4	29	26.1	23	20.7	6	13.6	6	23.1	73	21.9
Student satisfaction	3	5.2	16	5.8	6	3.6	13	8.2	4	9.5	5	4.5	8	7.2	0	0.0	2	7.7	19	5.7
Student-faculty interaction	3	5.2	40	14.4	16	9.6	27	17.0	4	9.5	16	14.4	16	14.4	4	9.1	3	11.5	43	12.9

Table continues on page 86

Table continued from page 85

Survey question/responses	Institution type				Institution control				Number of undergraduates enrolled											
	Two-year		Four-year		Public		Private		Fewer than 1,000		1,001 - 3,000		3,001 - 10,000		10,001 - 20,000		More than 20,000		Total	
	Freq.	%	Freq.	%	Freq.	%	Freq.	%	Freq.	%	Freq.	%	Freq.	%	Freq.	%	Freq.	%	Freq.	%
Q34. Please select the three most important objectives for this initiative: *(continued)*																				
Study skills	2	3.4	6	2.2	4	2.4	4	2.5	1	2.4	2	1.8	4	3.6	1	2.3	0	0.0	8	2.4
Support network or friendships	3	5.7	18	6.5	5	3.0	16	10.1	0	0.0	12	10.8	7	6.3	1	2.3	1	3.8	21	6.3
Writing skills	1	1.7	4	1.4	3	1.8	1	0.6	0	0.0	3	2.7	1	0.9	1	2.3	0	0.0	5	1.5
Other	8	13.8	15	5.4	13	7.8	8	5.0	4	9.5	7	6.3	4	3.6	7	15.9	1	3.8	23	6.9
Total	58	100.0	227	100.0	166	100.0	159	100.0	42	100.0	111	100.0	111	100.0	44	100.0	26	100.0	334	100.0
Q35. To what extent are each of the following elements present in this initiative? Performance expectations set at appropriately high levels.																				
1 - Element is not present	4	7.0	39	14.3	19	11.7	24	15.3	4	9.5	17	15.6	9	8.2	8	19.0	5	20.0	43	13.1
2	3	5.3	24	8.8	20	12.3	7	4.5	0	0.0	8	7.3	9	8.2	6	14.3	4	16.0	27	8.2
3 - Element is partially present	22	38.6	89	32.7	58	35.8	48	30.6	11	26.2	35	32.1	39	35.5	17	40.5	9	36.0	111	33.8
4	16	28.1	64	23.5	36	22.2	43	27.4	8	19.0	31	28.4	33	30.0	5	11.9	2	8.0	79	24.1
5 - Element is pervasive throughout initiative	12	21.1	56	20.6	29	17.9	35	22.3	19	45.2	18	16.5	20	18.2	6	14.3	5	20.0	68	20.7
Total	57	100.0	272	100.0	162	100.0	157	100.0	42	100.0	109	100.0	110	100.0	42	100.0	25	100.0	328	100.0
Q36. To what extent are each of the following elements present in this initiative? Significant investment of time and effort by students over an extended period of time.																				
1 - Element is not present	3	5.3	31	11.4	14	8.6	20	12.7	5	11.9	7	6.4	9	8.2	9	21.4	4	16.0	34	10.4
2	13	22.8	55	20.2	45	27.8	22	14.0	2	4.8	18	16.5	24	21.8	14	33.3	10	40.0	68	20.7
3 - Element is partially present	21	36.8	94	34.6	55	34.0	56	35.7	11	26.2	45	41.3	40	36.4	11	26.2	7	28.0	114	34.8
4	13	22.8	55	20.2	29	17.9	37	23.6	13	31.0	25	22.9	24	21.8	4	9.5	2	8.0	68	20.7
5 - Element is pervasive throughout initiative	7	12.3	37	13.6	19	11.7	22	14.0	11	26.2	14	12.8	13	11.8	4	9.5	2	8.0	44	13.4
Total	57	100.0	272	100.0	162	100.0	157	100.0	42	100.0	109	100.0	110	100.0	42	100.0	25	100.0	328	100.0

Table continues on page 87
Table continues on page 87

Table continued from page 86

Survey question/responses	Institution type				Institution control				Number of undergraduates enrolled										Total	
	Two-year		Four-year		Public		Private		Fewer than 1,000		1,001 - 3,000		3,001 - 10,000		10,001 - 20,000		More than 20,000			
	Freq.	%	Freq.	%	Freq.	%	Freq.	%	Freq.	%	Freq.	%	Freq.	%	Freq.	%	Freq.	%	Freq.	%
Q37. To what extent are each of the following elements present in this initiative? Interactions with faculty and peers about substantive matters.																				
1 - Element is not present	2	3.5	19	7.0	12	7.4	9	5.7	2	4.8	5	4.6	3	2.7	6	14.3	5	20.0	21	6.4
2	9	15.8	32	11.8	25	15.4	15	9.6	2	4.8	12	11.0	16	14.5	4	9.5	7	28.0	41	12.5
3 - Element is partially present	19	33.3	84	30.9	54	33.3	49	31.2	9	21.4	38	34.9	33	30.0	18	42.9	5	20.0	103	31.4
4	18	31.6	82	30.1	46	28.4	48	30.6	14	33.3	32	29.4	41	37.3	9	21.4	4	16.0	100	30.5
5 - Element is pervasive throughout initiative	9	15.8	55	20.2	25	15.4	36	22.9	15	35.7	22	20.2	17	15.5	5	11.9	4	16.0	63	19.2
Total	57	100.0	272	100.0	162	100.0	157	100.0	42	100.0	109	100	110	100.0	42	100.0	25	100.0	328	100.0
Q38. To what extent are each of the following elements present in this initiative? Experiences with diversity, wherein students are exposed to and must contend with people and circumstances that differ from those with which students are familiar.																				
1 - Element is not present	11	19.3	65	23.9	40	24.7	35	22.3	6	14.3	24	22.0	19	17.3	17	40.5	10	40.0	76	23.2
2	12	21.1	47	17.3	37	22.8	21	13.4	10	23.8	14	12.8	24	21.8	6	14.3	5	20.0	59	18.0
3 - Element is partially present	17	29.8	71	26.1	42	25.9	44	28.0	10	23.8	29	26.6	34	30.9	10	23.8	4	16.0	87	26.5
4	12	21.1	60	22.1	30	18.5	37	23.6	10	23.8	32	29.4	19	17.3	6	14.3	5	20.0	72	22.0
5 - Element is pervasive throughout initiative	5	8.8	29	10.7	13	8.0	20	12.7	6	14.3	10	9.2	14	12.7	3	7.1	1	4.0	34	10.4
Total	57	100.0	272	100.0	162	100.0	157	100.0	42	100.0	109	100	110	100.0	42	100.0	25	100.0	328	100.0
Q39. To what extent are each of the following elements present in this initiative? Frequent, timely, and constructive feedback.																				
1 - Element is not present	2	3.5	32	11.8	16	9.9	18	11.5	3	7.1	8	7.3	12	10.9	4	9.5	7	28.0	34	10.4
2	10	17.5	43	15.8	29	17.9	22	14.0	3	7.1	20	18.3	12	10.9	12	28.6	6	24.0	53	16.2
3 - Element is partially present	22	38.6	87	32.0	58	35.8	50	31.8	9	21.4	38	34.9	44	40.0	10	23.8	7	28.0	108	32.9
4	14	24.6	77	28.3	41	25.3	46	29.3	17	40.5	30	27.5	32	29.1	8	19.0	4	16.0	91	27.7
5 - Element is pervasive throughout initiative	9	15.8	33	12.1	18	11.1	21	13.4	10	23.8	13	11.9	10	9.1	8	19.0	1	4.0	42	12.8
Total	57	100.0	272	100.0	162	100.0	157	100.0	42	100.0	109	100.0	110	100.0	42	100.0	25	100	328	100.0

Table continues on page 88

Table continued from page 87

Survey question/responses	Institution type				Institution control				Number of undergraduates enrolled										Total	
	Two-year		Four-year		Public		Private		Fewer than 1,000		1,001 - 3,000		3,001 - 10,000		10,001 - 20,000		More than 20,000			
	Freq.	%	Freq.	%	Freq.	%	Freq.	%	Freq.	%	Freq.	%	Freq.	%	Freq.	%	Freq.	%	Freq.	%
Q40. To what extent are each of the following elements present in this initiative? Periodic, structured opportunities to reflect and integrate learning.																				
1 - Element is not present	8	14.0	43	15.8	27	16.7	24	15.3	6	14.3	14	12.8	11	10.0	14	33.3	6	24.0	51	15.5
2	9	15.8	53	19.5	40	24.7	20	12.7	1	2.4	17	15.6	23	20.9	10	23.8	11	44.0	62	18.9
3 - Element is partially present	20	35.1	72	26.5	48	29.6	42	26.8	11	26.2	35	32.1	34	30.9	7	16.7	5	20.0	92	28.0
4	14	24.6	63	23.2	34	21.0	41	26.1	11	26.2	29	26.6	26	23.6	9	21.4	1	4.0	76	23.2
5 - Element is pervasive throughout initiative	6	10.5	41	15.1	13	8.0	30	19.1	13	31.0	14	12.8	16	14.5	2	4.8	2	8.0	47	14.3
Total	57	100.0	272	100.0	162	100.0	157	100.0	42	100.0	109	100.0	110	100.0	42	100.0	25	100.0	328	100.0
Q41. To what extent are each of the following elements present in this initiative? Opportunities to discover relevance of learning through real-world applications.																				
1 - Element is not present	7	12.3	58	21.3	36	22.2	29	18.5	8	19.0	17	15.6	12	10.9	18	42.9	10	40.0	65	19.8
2	11	19.3	45	16.5	36	22.2	19	12.1	2	4.8	15	13.8	26	23.6	4	9.5	8	32.0	55	16.8
3 - Element is partially present	20	35.1	84	30.9	49	30.2	51	32.5	12	28.6	38	34.9	40	36.4	11	26.2	3	12.0	104	31.7
4	9	15.8	55	20.2	25	15.4	36	22.9	7	16.7	28	25.7	20	18.2	7	16.7	2	8.0	64	19.5
5 - Element is pervasive throughout initiative	10	17.5	30	11.0	16	9.9	22	14.0	13	31.0	11	10.1	12	10.9	2	4.8	2	8.0	40	12.2
Total	57	100.0	272	100.0	162	100.0	157	100.0	42	100.0	109	100.0	110	100.0	42	100.0	25	100.0	328	100.0
Q42. To what extent are each of the following elements present in this initiative? Public demonstration of competence.																				
1 - Element is not present	13	22.8	110	40.4	61	37.7	62	39.5	16	38.1	36	33.0	30	27.3	24	57.1	17	68.0	123	37.5
2	14	24.6	52	19.1	35	21.6	28	17.8	5	11.9	20	18.3	28	25.5	8	19.0	4	16.0	65	19.8
3 - Element is partially present	16	28.1	59	21.7	36	22.2	37	23.6	9	21.4	29	26.6	30	27.3	7	16.7	0	0.0	75	22.9
4	7	12.3	35	12.9	19	11.7	21	13.4	4	9.5	18	16.5	16	14.5	1	2.4	3	12.0	42	12.8
5 - Element is pervasive throughout initiative	7	12.3	16	5.9	11	6.8	9	5.7	8	19.0	6	5.5	6	5.5	2	4.8	1	4.0	23	7.0
Total	57	100.0	272	100.0	162	100.0	157	100.0	42	100.0	109	100.0	110	100.0	42	100.0	25	100.0	328	100.0

Table continues on page 89

Table continued from page 88

Survey question/responses	Two-year Freq.	Two-year %	Four-year Freq.	Four-year %	Public Freq.	Public %	Private Freq.	Private %	Fewer than 1,000 Freq.	Fewer than 1,000 %	1,001-3,000 Freq.	1,001-3,000 %	3,001-10,000 Freq.	3,001-10,000 %	10,001-20,000 Freq.	10,001-20,000 %	More than 20,000 Freq.	More than 20,000 %	Total Freq.	Total %
Q43. Which campus unit directly administers this initiative?																				
Academic affairs central office	18	31.6	66	24.3	42	25.9	40	25.5	13	31.0	33	30.3	21	19.1	9	21.4	8	32.0	84	25.6
College or school (e.g., College of Liberal Arts)	2	3.5	28	10.3	22	13.6	7	4.5	1	2.4	2	1.8	11	10.0	9	21.4	6	24.0	29	8.8
Academic department(s), please specify:	7	12.3	35	12.9	21	13.0	17	10.8	7	16.7	14	12.8	16	14.5	3	7.1	2	8.0	42	12.8
Second-year program office	0	0.0	5	1.8	2	1.2	3	1.9	1	2.4	2	1.8	1	0.9	0	0.0	1	4.0	5	1.5
Student affairs central office	9	15.8	17	6.3	10	6.2	16	10.2	7	16.7	11	10.1	4	3.6	4	9.5	0	0.0	26	7.9
Student affairs unit, please specify:	13	22.8	72	26.5	37	22.8	47	29.9	8	19.0	30	27.5	36	32.7	7	16.7	4	16.0	85	25.9
Other	8	14.0	49	18.0	28	17.3	27	17.2	5	11.9	17	15.6	21	19.1	10	23.8	4	16.0	57	17.4
Total	57	100.0	272	100.0	162	100.0	157	100.0	42	100.0	109	100.0	110	100.0	42	100.0	25	100.0	328	100.0
Q44. How is the initiative primarily funded?																				
Auxiliary funds—non-tuition-basec fees and services	2	3.5	34	12.5	14	8.6	22	14.0	2	4.8	11	10.1	15	13.6	5	11.9	3	12.0	36	11.0
Foundation funds	1	1.8	1	0.4	1	0.6	0	0.0	2	4.8	0	0.0	0	0.0	0	0.0	0	0.0	2	0.6
Grant funds	6	10.5	18	6.6	14	8.6	9	5.7	6	14.3	8	7.3	5	4.5	2	4.8	3	12.0	24	7.3
Nonrecurring or one-time funds	0	0.0	4	1.5	2	1.2	2	1.3	0	0.0	2	1.8	0	0.0	2	4.8	0	0.0	4	1.2
Recurring state- or university-appropriated funds	30	52.6	111	40.8	89	54.9	49	31.2	12	28.6	36	33.0	52	47.3	25	59.5	15	60.0	140	42.7
Student activity fees	4	7.0	20	7.4	14	8.6	10	6.4	4	9.5	7	6.4	8	7.3	3	7.1	2	3.0	24	7.3
Other	14	24.6	84	30.9	28	17.3	65	41.4	16	38.1	45	41.3	30	27.3	5	11.9	2	3.0	98	29.9
Total	57	100.0	272	100.0	162	100.0	157	100.0	42	100.0	109	100.0	110	100.0	42	100.0	25	100.0	328	100.0

Table continues on page 90

Table continued from page 89

Survey question/responses	Institution type				Institution control				Number of undergraduates enrolled										Total	
	Two-year		Four-year		Public		Private		Fewer than 1,000		1,001 - 3,000		3,001 - 10,000		10,001 - 20,000		More than 20,000			
	Freq.	%	Freq.	%	Freq.	%	Freq.	%	Freq.	%	Freq.	%	Freq.	%	Freq.	%	Freq.	%	Freq.	%
Q47. Please identify the national survey(s) you used: (Select all that apply.)																				
College Student Experiences Questionnaire (CSEQ)	0	0.0	0	0.0	0	0.0	0	0.0	0	0.0	0	0.0	0	0.0	0	0.0	0	0.0	0	0.0
Collegiate Learning Assessment (CLA)	0	0.0	7	19.4	1	5.3	6	28.6	1	33.3	3	21.4	3	16.7	0	0.0	0	0.0	7	17.1
Community College Survey of Student Engagement (CCSSE)	4	80.0	0	0.0	4	21.1	0	0.0	0	0.0	1	7.1	1	5.6	2	50.0	0	0.0	4	9.8
Faculty Survey of Student Engagement (FSSE)	0	0.0	2	5.6	2	10.5	0	0.0	0	0.0	0	0.0	2	11.1	0	0.0	0	0.0	2	4.9
Individual Development and Educational Assessment (IDEA)	0	0.0	2	5.6	1	5.3	1	4.8	1	33.3	0	0.0	1	5.6	0	0.0	0	0.0	2	4.9
National Survey of Student Engagement (NSSE)	0	0.0	27	75.0	12	63.2	15	71.4	3	100.0	8	57.1	13	72.2	1	25.0	2	100.0	27	65.9
Second-Year Student Assessment	2	40.0	8	22.2	4	21.1	6	28.6	1	33.3	2	14.3	6	33.3	1	25.0	0	0.0	10	24.4
Sophomore Experiences Survey	0	0.0	0	0.0	0	0.0	0	0.0	0	0.0	0	0.0	0	0.0	0	0.0	0	0.0	0	0.0
Student Satisfaction Inventory (SSI)	2	40.0	16	44.0	5	26.3	13	61.9	2	66.7	9	64.3	6	33.3	1	25.0	0	0.0	18	43.9
Other	1	20.0	10	27.8	5	26.3	5	23.8	0	0.0	4	28.6	6	33.3	0	0.0	1	50.0	11	26.8
Total	5	100.0	36	100.0	19	100.0	21	100.0	3	100.0	14	100.0	18	100.0	4	100.0	2	100.0	41	100.0

Appendix D: Survey Instrument: Sophomore Experiences Survey[a]

Sophomore Experiences Survey

In order to better understand the experiences of students in their second year of college, we would like for you to please respond to each of the sections below. No individual identifying information is requested of you and all responses will be grouped with other students before being reported. Thank you for taking the time to complete the survey—it should only take you 15-20 minutes or so.

1. Is this your second year attending college?

   ❏ Yes

   ❏ No

2. How many college credits/units do you have, including this term's courses? _____

3. How many credits are you taking this term?_____

4. Did you transfer to this institution from another university?

   ❏ Yes

   ❏ No

5. If you transferred here, how long ago did you do so?

   ❏ Within the last 3 months

   ❏ 3-6 months ago

   ❏ 7-12 months ago

   ❏ 13-18 months ago

   ❏ More than 18 months ago

Think about the classes you are taking RIGHT NOW – this term – as you answer the following questions.

6. Please rate your agreement with each of the items by using a 1 to 6 scale, with 1 indicating *strongly disagree* and 6 indicating *strongly agree*.

	Strongly Disagree 1	2	3	4	5	Strongly Agree 6
I feel as though I am learning things in my classes that are worthwhile to me as a person.						
I can usually find ways of applying what I'm learning in class to something else in my life.						
I am confident I will reach my educational goals.						
I find a way to get everything done for classes that I need to do in a given week.						
I find myself thinking about what I'm learning in class even when I'm not in class.						
Once I start a project, I stick with it until I'm finished.						
Even if assignments are not interesting to me, I find a way to keep working at them until they are done well.						
I feel energized by the ideas I am learning in most of my classes.						
I know how to apply my strengths to achieve academic success.						
I am bored in class a lot of the time.						
I am good at juggling all the demands of college life.						
Other people would say I'm a hard worker.						
I feel like I belong here.						
Other people seem to make friends more easily than I do.						
Being a student here fills an important need in my life.						
I find the relationships in my life difficult.						
I spend time making a difference in other people's lives.						
Students have a voice in what happens on this campus.						
I feel proud of the college or university I have chosen to attend.						
My family approves of me attending this institution.						
I don't have as many close friends as I wish I had.						
My family encourages me to complete my degree.						
There is a strong sense of community on this campus.						
My close friends encourage me to continue attending this school.						
I know I can make a difference in my community.						
There are people in my life who are willing to listen when I need to talk.						
My spiritual or religious beliefs provide me with a sense of strength when life is difficult.						
When I'm faced with a problem in my life, I can usually think of several ways to solve it.						
My perspective on life is that I tend to see the glass as "half full."						
College life is excellent for me.						
It's hard to make friends on this campus.						
I believe I have a bright future.						

	Strongly Disagree 1	2	3	4	5	Strongly Agree 6
I have found a major that is a good fit for me.						
I gain spiritual strength by trusting in a higher power beyond myself.						
Life is good for me right now.						
I speak up for those who cannot speak for themselves.						
There is a strong sense of community among students in my major.						
My spiritual or religious beliefs are the foundation of my approach to life.						
It's important for me to make a contribution to my community.						
I am confident that the amount of money I'm paying for college is worth it in the long run.						
I intend to re-enroll at this institution next year.						
I intend to graduate from this institution.						
Given my current goals, this institution is a good fit for me.						
If I had to do it over again, I would choose a different university to attend.						
I really enjoy being a student here.						

7. Please rate your level of participation in each of the following activities this semester:

	Never 1	2	3	4	5	Frequently 6
Student organizations on campus						
Campus events or activities						
Leadership of student organizations						
Interaction with faculty outside of class						
Music or theater performance groups on campus						
Fraternity/sorority						
Community service						
Religious services or activities						
Campus ethnic organizations (such as Black Student Association)						

8. How often have you engaged in each of the following THIS YEAR?

	Never 1	2	3	4	5	Frequently 6
Met with a professor during office hours						
Discussed career plans or goals with a professor						
Met informally or socially with a faculty member outside of class or office hours						
Discussed academic issues with a faculty member outside of class or office hours						
Met with your academic advisor						
Attended any programs geared specifically to sophomores						

9. Rate your satisfaction with each of the following aspects of your college experience using a 1 to 6 scale, with 1 indicating very dissatisfied and 6 indicating very satisfied.

	Very Dissatisfied 1	2	3	4	5	Very Dissatisfied 6
The amount you are learning in your classes THIS TERM						
The grades you are earning so far THIS TERM						
The academic advising you have experienced THIS YEAR						
Your overall experiences on this campus THIS YEAR						
The amount of contact you have had with faculty THIS YEAR						
The quality of the interaction you have had with faculty THIS YEAR						
Your experiences with your peers on this campus THIS YEAR						
Your current living situation						
Your current level of physical health						
The amount of money you personally have to pay to attend college here						
Faculty sensitivity to the needs of diverse students						
Your interactions with the people with whom you share your living space						

Please tell us a little about yourself. Your answers will be grouped with those of other students to help us understand our students better. No individual information will be reported for any reason.

10. Are you the first in your immediate family to attend college?

❒ Yes

❒ No

11. What is your sex?

❒ Female

❒ Male

12. What is your age? _____

13. What is the highest degree you see yourself obtaining at some point in your life?

❒ Associate's degree

❒ Bachelor's degree

❒ Teaching credential

❒ Master's degree

❒ Doctorate

❒ Medical or law degree

❒ Other (please specify) _____

14. How would you describe your grades in high school?

- ❏ Mostly *As*
- ❏ *As* and *Bs*
- ❏ Mostly *Bs*
- ❏ *Bs* and *Cs*
- ❏ Mostly *Cs*
- ❏ *Cs* and *Ds*
- ❏ *Ds* and *Fs*

15. How would you describe your grades in your first year of college?

- ❏ Mostly *As*
- ❏ *As* and *Bs*
- ❏ Mostly *Bs*
- ❏ *Bs* and *Cs*
- ❏ Mostly *Cs*
- ❏ *Cs* and *Ds*
- ❏ *Ds* and *Fs*

16. How would you describe your grades THIS YEAR?

- ❏ Mostly *As*
- ❏ *As* and *Bs*
- ❏ Mostly *Bs*
- ❏ *Bs* and *Cs*
- ❏ Mostly *Cs*
- ❏ *Cs* and *Ds*
- ❏ *Ds* and *Fs*

17. When you chose to attend this institution, was it your first choice?

- ❏ Yes
- ❏ No

18. Where do you live?

- ❏ On campus
- ❏ Off campus
- ❏ Other (Please specify.)_____

19. Are you a student athlete?

- ❏ Yes
- ❏ No

20. What is your race or ethnicity?

❐ African American/Black

❐ American Indian/Alaskan Native

❐ Asian American/Asian

❐ Caucasian/White

❐ Latino/Hispanic

❐ International

❐ Prefer not to respond

21. How many hours per week do you work OFF campus?

❐ None

❐ 5 or less

❐ 6-10 hours

❐ 11-15 hours

❐ 16-20 hours

❐ 21-25 hours

❐ 26-30 hours

❐ More than 30 hours

22. How many hours per week do you work ON campus?

❐ None

❐ 5 or less

❐ 6-10 hours

❐ 11-15 hours

❐ 16-20 hours

❐ 21-25 hours

❐ 26-30 hours

❐ More than 30 hours

23. What is your major? (Leave blank if you have not declared a major yet) _____

24. How sure are you of your major?

❐ Very unsure

❐ Unsure

❐ Somewhat unsure

❐ Somewhat sure

❐ Sure

❐ Very sure

25. How often have you participated in service-learning COURSES in college?

- ❏ Not at all
- ❏ One course
- ❏ More than one course

26. Have you participated in a learning community in college? (*A learning community is defined as two or more courses that you take in a block with the same group of students. It may or may not also involve your residence hall*).

- ❏ Yes
- ❏ No
- ❏ Not sure

27. How many courses have you dropped or withdrawn from since beginning college? (count all courses taken at any college)

- ❏ None
- ❏ 1
- ❏ 2-3
- ❏ 4-5
- ❏ 6 or more

28. In how many courses have you received a grade below C since beginning college? (count all colleges attended)

- ❏ None
- ❏ 1
- ❏ 2-3
- ❏ 4-5
- ❏ 6 or more

29. Have you traveled outside the United States since entering college?

- ❏ No
- ❏ For two weeks or less
- ❏ For more than two weeks

30. Compared to your first year of college, this year has been:

- ❏ Much worse
- ❏ Worse
- ❏ About the same
- ❏ Better
- ❏ Much better

31. Compared to the courses you took in your first year of college, have your courses this year been:

❑ Much worse

❑ Worse

❑ About the same

❑ Better

❑ Much better

32. How many of your courses THIS YEAR have been taught by adjunct or part-time faculty?

❑ None

❑ 1

❑ 2-3

❑ 4-5

❑ 6 or more

33. How much time each week do you spend on the following activities? Please rate your time commitment using a 1 to 6 scale, with

1 = *never*

2 = *less than one hour per week*

3 = *1-7 hours per week*

4 = *8-14 hours per week*

5 = *15-21 hours per week*

6 = *more than 21 hours per week*

	Never 1	2	3	4	5	More than 21 hours/ week 6
Studying for classes						
Online social networking (e.g., Facebook, Twitter)						
Playing Internet or video games						
Watching TV						
Hanging out with friends						

34. How often do you call or text home (parents or spouse/children) while you are on campus?

❑ Never

❑ Once a week or less

❑ 2-3 times a week or so

❑ About once a day

❑ 2-3 times a day

❑ 4 or more times a day

35. How often do you get less than four hours of sleep in a night?

   ❏ Never

   ❏ Rarely

   ❏ Occasionally

   ❏ Fairly often

   ❏ Frequently

   ❏ Almost always

36. Considering the financial aid you have received and the money you and your family have, how much difficulty have you had so far in paying for your school expenses?

   ❏ No difficulty

   ❏ A little difficulty

   ❏ Some difficulty

   ❏ A fair amount of difficulty

   ❏ Great difficulty

37. We are interested in what helps students thrive in college. Thriving is defined as getting the most out of your college experience, so that you are intellectually, socially, and psychologically engaged and enjoying the college experience. Given that definition, to what extent do you think you are thriving as a college student this semester?

   ❏ Not even surviving

   ❏ Barely surviving

   ❏ Surviving

   ❏ Somewhat thriving

   ❏ Thriving most of the time

   ❏ Consistently thriving

38. Please add anything else you think is important for us to know about your experiences in your second year of college. For instance, if there was one thing you could change about this year, what would it be? _____

Thank you for taking the time to give us your perspective. When combined with the responses of other students from around the country, they will provide important feedback to colleges and universities about how to meet the needs of students in the second year of college. Thank you!

Appendix E: National Norms for the Sophomore Experiences Survey

Table E.1

Thriving Quotient Subscales and Items

Item	Mean	SD
Engaged learning		
I feel as though I am learning things in my classes that are worthwhile to me as a person.	4.73	1.06
I can usually find ways of applying what I'm learning in class to something else in my life.	4.65	1.05
I find myself thinking about what I'm learning in class even when I'm not in class.	4.52	1.14
I feel energized by the ideas I'm learning in most of my classes.	4.26	1.15
Academic determination		
I am confident I will reach my educational goals.	5.07	0.98
Even if assignments are not interesting to me, I find a way to keep working at them until they are done well.	4.61	1.09
I know how to apply my strengths to achieve academic success.	4.87	0.96
I am good at juggling all the demands of college life.	4.57	1.10
Other people would say I'm a hard worker.	5.02	0.99
When I'm faced with a problem in my life, I can usually think of several ways to solve it.	4.77	0.87
Social connectedness		
Other people seem to make friends more easily than I do.	3.57	0.99
I don't have as many close friends as I wish I had.	3.35	1.59
I feel like my friends really care about me.	4.99	0.99
I feel content with the kinds of friendships I currently have.	4.82	1.05
It's hard to make friends on this campus.	3.06	1.41
I often feel lonely because I have few close friends with whom to share my concerns.	3.04	1.53
Diverse citizenship		
I spend time making a difference in other people's lives.	4.53	1.05
I value interacting with people whose viewpoints are different from my own.	4.63	0.96
I know I can make a difference in my community.	4.72	0.98
It is important to become aware of the perspectives of individuals from different backgrounds.	5.13	0.89
It's important for me to make a contribution to my community.	4.83	0.97
My knowledge or opinions have been influenced or changed by becoming more aware of the perspectives of individuals from different backgrounds.	4.77	1.03

Table E.1 continues on page 102

Table E.1 continued from page 101

Item	Mean	SD
Positive perspective		
When things are uncertain, I tend to expect the worst.	3.87	1.37
My perspective on life is that I tend to see the glass as "half full" rather than "half empty."	4.53	1.14
I look for the best in situations, even when things seem hopeless.	4.63	1.03
Psychological sense of community		
I feel like I belong here.	4.77	1.23
Being a student here fills an important need in my life.	4.76	1.14
I feel proud of the college or university I have chosen to attend.	4.86	1.13
There is a strong sense of community on this campus.	4.34	1.20
Spirituality		
My spiritual or religious beliefs provide me with a sense of strength when life is difficult.	4.25	1.60
My spiritual or religious beliefs are the foundation of my approach to life.	3.77	1.67
My spiritual or religious beliefs give meaning and purpose to my life.	4.18	1.62
My life has a purpose because I am part of something greater than myself.	4.71	1.14
I have a good sense of what makes my life meaningful.	4.88	0.98
I am searching for something that makes my life feel significant.	3.93	1.44
I am looking for something that makes my life meaningful.	4.04	1.39
Outcome measures	3.06	1.41
I am confident that the amount of money I'm paying for college is worth it in the long run.	3.04	1.53
I intend to re-enroll at this institution next year.		
I intend to graduate from this institution.	4.53	1.05
Given my current goals, this institution is a good fit for me.	4.63	0.96
If I had to do it over again, I would choose a different institution.	4.72	0.98
I really enjoy being a student here.	5.13	0.89

Note. Items are on a 6-point scale indicating agreement or disagreement with each statement with 6 indicating *strongly agree.*

Table E.2
Student Involvement Items

Type of activity	Never 1 %	2 %	3 %	4 %	5 %	Frequently 6 %
Student organizations on campus	15.3	13.3	14.1	18.2	15.4	23.7
Campus events or activities	8.9	12.3	19.1	25.5	18.6	15.7
Leadership of student organizations	35.1	16.1	12.0	12.5	10.2	14.2
Fraternity/sorority	71.2	6.3	3.6	3.5	3.1	12.3
Community service	23.0	16.4	15.9	16.8	13.5	14.4
Religious services on or off campus	44.1	12.3	10.4	10.6	9.3	13.3
Campus ethnic organizations	70.6	11.6	5.9	4.7	3.0	4.2
Attended any programs geared specifically to sophomores	51.5	16.4	11.0	9.0	5.7	6.4

Table E.3
Faculty-Student Interaction Items

Type of activity	Never 1 %	2 %	3 %	4 %	5 %	Frequently 6 %
Interaction with faculty outside of class	12.7	19.2	20.8	20.6	14.5	12.3
Met with a professor during office hours	11.9	14.1	16.8	23.4	16.5	17.3
Discussed career plans or goals with a professor	18.3	14.7	15.8	20.6	15.8	14.9
Met informally or socially with a faculty member outside of class or office hours	44.9	14.8	10.1	12.4	9.2	8.5
Discussed academic issues with a faculty member outside of class or office hours	36.0	15.7	12.0	14.7	11.6	10.0
Met with your academic advisor	5.2	12.1	17.1	22.5	21.3	21.8

Table E.4
Satisfaction Items

Satisfaction with:	Very dissatisfied %	Dissatisfied %	Somewhat dissatisfied %	Somewhat satisfied %	Satisfied %	Very satisfied %
The amount you are learning in your classes this term	1.2	3.0	6.6	23.3	47.8	18.0
The grades you are earning so far this term	2.8	5.7	11.4	30.3	34.8	14.9
The academic advising you have received this year	4.6	6.4	9.3	23.1	33.3	23.4
Your overall experiences on this campus so far	1.8	2.7	7.8	23.1	43.5	21.1
The amount of contact you have had with faculty this year	1.2	3.5	9.1	29.1	40.8	16.3
The quality of interaction you have had with faculty this year	1.3	3.2	8.3	27.0	42.2	18.0
Your experiences with your peers on this campus this year	1.8	3.1	7.9	21.4	41.6	24.3
Your current living situation.	4.9	6.1	9.3	20.5	34.9	24.3
Your current level of physical health	2.4	5.3	10.7	24.2	37.1	20.3
The amount of money you personally have to pay to attend college here	16.4	17.2	18.6	20.7	16.7	10.4
Faculty sensitivity to the needs of diverse students	2.5	3.8	11.6	31.5	37.3	13.3

Table E.5
Sophomore Student Characteristics

Characteristic	%
Demographic information	
First in immediate family to attend college	22.5
Enrolled full time	98.4
Enrolled in the Honors College or Honors Program on campus	12.0
Live on campus	55.5
Transferred into the institution	
Institution was first choice at enrollment	63.3
Student athlete	9.0
Gender	
Female	71.4
Male	28.2
Other	0.4
Age	
17 or younger	0.2
18-20	90.3
21-23	7.0
24-26	0.8
27-30	0.6
31-34	0.3
35-38	0.2
38-42	0.1
43-46	0.1
47-50	0.2
Over 50	0.2
Degree aspirations	
Associate's degree	1.2
Bachelor's degree	28.6
Teaching credential	2.1
Master's degree	43.8
Doctorate	15.6
Medical or law degree	8.7
Other	
Ethnicity	
African American/Black	8.4
American Indian/Alaskan Native	1.3
Asian American/Asian/Pacific Islander	4.3
Caucasian/White	63.1
Latino/Hispanic	6.2
International	1.3
Prefer not to respond	15.4

Table E.5 continues on page 105

Table E.5 continued from page 104

Characteristic	%
Family income	
Less than $30,000 a year	16.6
$30,000-$59,999	23.6
$60,000-$89,999	26.6
$90,000-$119,99	18.0
$120,000 and over	15.1
Work for pay	
No	35.7
On campus	22.8
Off campus	33.5
Both on and off campus	8.1
High school grades	
Mostly *As*	37.2
Mostly *As* and *Bs*	43.1
Mostly *Bs*	10.1
Mostly *Bs* and *Cs*	7.5
Mostly *Cs*	1.3
Below a *C* average	0.5
First-year grades	
Mostly *As*	29.5
Mostly *As* and *Bs*	37.1
Mostly *Bs*	15.3
Mostly *Bs* and *Cs*	13.1
Mostly *Cs*	2.9
Below a *C* average	1.8
Ds and *Fs*	0.3
Second-year grades	
Mostly *As*	26.1
Mostly *As* and *Bs*	40.7
Mostly *Bs*	16.9
Mostly *Bs* and *Cs*	12.5
Mostly *Cs*	3.0
Below a *C* average	0.8
Ds and *Fs*	0.1
Courses received grade below C	
None	59.4
One	17.5
Two or three	18.7
Four or five	4.0
Six or more	0.5

Table E.5 continues on page 106

Table E.5 continued from page 105

Characteristic	%
Courses dropped	
None	57.4
One	26.5
Two or three	14.0
Four or five	1.5
Six or more	0.6
Certainty of major	
Very unsure	3.5
Unsure	2.2
Somewhat unsure	4.2
Somewhat sure	11.9
Sure	27.8
Very sure	50.2
Participation in service-learning courses	
Never	77.7
One course	16.9
More than one course	5.4
Participation in a learning community	
Yes	19.4
No	62.8
Not sure	17.9
Traveled outside United States since entering college	
No	77.3
Two weeks or less	15.1
More than two weeks	7.6
Sophomore courses taught by adjunct or part-time faculty	
None	29.2
One	23.9
Two or three	2.3
Four or five	0.6
Six or more	0.0
Participated in research with faculty	
Yes	15.3
No	84.7
Comparison to first year of college	
Much worse	3.7
Worse	14.0
About the same	33.1
Better	33.6
Much better	15.6

Table E.5 continues on page 107

Table E.5 continued from page 106

Characteristic	%
Courses compared to first year of college	
Much worse	3.8
Worse	17.2
About the same	37.6
Better	30.3
Much better	11.0
Difficulty in paying for school expenses	
No difficulty	21.8
A little difficulty	27.8
Some difficulty	26.8
A fair amount of difficulty	15.6
Great difficulty	8.0
Overall thriving	
Not even surviving	1.0
Barely surviving	6.4
Surviving	19.9
Somewhat thriving	28.1
Thriving most of the time	35.3
Consistently thriving	9.1

References

Astin, A. W. (1991). *Assessment for excellence.* Phoenix, AZ: American Council on Education/Oryx.

Barefoot, B. O., Griffin, B. Q., & Koch, A. K. (2012). *Enhancing student success and retention throughout undergraduate education: A national survey.* Brevard, NC: John N. Gardner Institute for Excellence in Undergraduate Education.

Baxter Magolda, M. B., King, P. M., Taylor, K. B., & Wakefield, K. M. (2012). Decreasing authority dependence during the first year of college. *Journal of College Student Development, 53*(3), 418-435.

Boyer Commission on Educating Undergraduates in the Research University. (1998). *Reinventing undergraduate education: A blueprint for America's research universities.* Stony Brook, NY: State University of New York.

Braxton, J. M., Hirschy, A. S., & McClendon, S. A. (2004). *Toward understanding and reducing college student departure* (ASHE-ERIC Higher Education Research Report Series No. 30). San Francisco, CA: Jossey-Bass.

Coburn, K. L., & Treeger, M. L. (1997). *Letting go: A parent's guide to understanding the college years.* New York, NY: Harper-Collins.

Freedman, M. B. (1956). The passage through college. *Journal of Social Issues, 12*(4), 13–28.

Gahagan, J., & Hunter, M. S. (2006). The second-year experience: Turning attention to the academy's middle children. *About Campus, 11*(3), 17-22.

Gahagan, J., & Hunter, M. S. (2010). Residential learning in the sophomore year. In M. S. Hunter, B. F. Tobolowsky, J. N. Gardner, S. E. Evenbeck, J. A. Pattengale, M. A. Schaller, & L. A. Schreiner (Eds.), *Helping sophomores succeed: Understanding and improving the second-year experience* (pp. 189-202). San Francisco, CA: Jossey-Bass.

Gardner, J. N., Pattengale, J. A., Tobolowsky, B. F., & Hunter, M. S. (2010). Introduction. In M. S. Hunter, B. F. Tobolowsky, J. N. Gardner, S. E. Evenbeck, J. A. Pattengale, M. A. Schaller, & L. A. Schreiner (Eds.), *Helping sophomores succeed: Understanding and improving the second-year experience* (pp. 1-10). San Francisco, CA: Jossey-Bass.

Gardner, P. D. (2000). From drift to engagement: Finding purpose and making career connections in the sophomore year. In L. A. Schreiner & J. Pattengale (Eds.) *Visible solutions for invisible students: Helping sophomores succeed* (Monograph No. 31, pp. 67-77). Columbia, SC: University of South Carolina, National Resource Center for The First Year Experience & Students in Transition.

Gordon, V. N. (2010). Academic advising: Helping sophomores succeed. In M. S. Hunter, B. F. Tobolowsky, J. N. Gardner, S. E. Evenbeck, J. A. Pattengale, M. A. Schaller, & L. A. Schreiner (Eds.), *Helping sophomores succeed: Understanding and improving the second-year experience* (pp. 83-98). San Francisco, CA: Jossey-Bass.

Graunke. S. S., & Woosley, S. A. (2005). An exploration of the factors that affect the academic success of college sophomores. *College Student Journal, 39*(2), 367-376.

Gunn, H. (2002, December). Web-based surveys: Changing the survey process. *First Monday, 7*(12). doi:10.5210/fm.v7i12.1014

Higher Education Research Institute (HERI). (2003). *College Students' Beliefs and Values Survey.* Retrieved from http://heri.ucla.edu/researchers/instruments/CIRP/2003SIF-CSBV.PDF

Jones, S. G., & Franco, R. W. (2010). Service-learning in the sophomore year. In M. S. Hunter, B. F. Tobolowsky, J. N. Gardner, S. E. Evenbeck, J. A. Pattengale, M. A. Schaller, & L. A. Schreiner (Eds.), *Helping sophomores succeed: Understanding and improving the second-year experience* (pp. 146-162). San Francisco, CA: Jossey-Bass.

Keeling, R. (Ed.). (2004). *Learning reconsidered: A campus-wide focus on the student experience.* Washington, DC: National Association of Student Personnel Administrators & American College Personnel Association.

Kennedy, K., & Upcraft, M. L. (2010). Keys to student success: A look at the literature. In M. S. Hunter, B. F. Tobolowsky, J. N. Gardner, S. E. Evenbeck, J. A. Pattengale, M. A. Schaller, & L. A. Schreiner (Eds.), *Helping sophomores succeed: Understanding and improving the second-year experience* (pp. 30-42). San Francisco, CA: Jossey-Bass.

Keup, J. R., Gahagan, J., & Goodwin, R. N. (2010). *2008 National Survey of Sophomore-Year Initiatives: Curricular and co-curricular structures supporting the success of second-year students* (Research Reports on College Transitions No. 1). Columbia, SC: University of South Carolina, National Resource Center for The First-Year Experience & Students in Transition.

Kuh, G. D. (2008). *High-impact educational practices: What they are, who has access to them, and why they matter.* Washington, DC: Association of American Colleges & Universities.

Kuh, G. D. (2010). High-impact practices: Retrospective and prospective. In J. E. Brownell & L. E. Swaner, *Five high-impact practices: Research on learning outcomes, completion, and quality.* (pp. v-xiii). Washington, DC: Association of American Colleges & Universities.

Kuh, G. D. (2013). Taking HIPs to the next level. In G. D. Kuh & K. O'Donnell, *Ensuring quality and taking high-impact practices to scale* (pp. 1-14). Washington, DC: Association of American Colleges & Universities.

Kuh, G. D., Kinzie, J., Schuh, J. H., Whitt, E. J., & Associates. (2005). *Student success in college: Creating conditions that matter.* San Francisco, CA: Jossey-Bass.

Leigh, D. E., & Gill, A. M. (2003). Do community colleges really divert students from earning bachelor's degrees? *Economics of Education Review, 22,* 23-30.

Lipka, S. (2006, September 8). After the freshman bubble pops: More colleges try to help their sophomores thrive. *Chronicle of Higher Education,* A34.

Lounsbury, J., & DeNeui, D. (1995). Psychological sense of community on campus. *College Student Journal, 29,* 270-277.

Margolis, G. (1989). Developmental opportunities. In P. A. Graysen & K. Cauley (Eds.), *College psychotherapy* (pp. 71-91). New York, NY: Guilford Press.

McIntosh, E. J. (2015) Thriving and spirituality: Making meaning out of the meaning making for students of color. *About Campus, 19*(6), 16-23.

McMillan, D. W., & Chavis, D. M. (1986). Sense of community: A definition and theory. *Journal of Community Psychology, 14,* 6-23.

National Center for Education Statistics. (2014). *Integrated postsecondary education data system* [Data file]. Retrieved from http://nces.ed.gov/ipeds

Noel-Levitz. (2013). *2013 student retention indicators benchmark report for four-year and two-year institutions.* Coralville, IA: Author. Retrieved from www.noellevitz.com/BenchmarkReports

Pattengale, J., & Schreiner, L. A. (2000). What is the sophomore slump and why should we care? In L. A. Schreiner & J. Pattengale (Eds.), *Visible solutions for invisible students: Helping sophomores succeed* (Monograph No. 31, pp. v-vii). Columbia, SC: University of South Carolina, National Resource Center for The First-Year Experience and Students in Transition.

Sarason, S. B. (1974). *The psychological sense of community: Prospects for a community psychology.* San Francisco, CA: Jossey-Bass.

Schaller, M. A. (2005). Wandering and wondering: Traversing the uneven terrain of the second college year. *About Campus, 10*(3), 17-24.

Schaller, M. A. (2010). Understanding the impact of the second year of college. In M. S. Hunter, B. F. Tobolowsky, J. N. Gardner, S. E. Evenbeck, J. A. Pattengale, M. A. Schaller, & L. A. Schreiner (Eds.), *Helping sophomores succeed: Understanding and improving the second-year experience* (pp. 13-29). San Francisco, CA: Jossey-Bass.

Schreiner, L. A. (2010a). The "Thriving Quotient": A new vision for student success. *About Campus, 15*(2), 2-10.

Schreiner, L. A. (2010b). Thriving in the classroom. *About Campus, 15*(3), 1-9.

Schreiner, L. A. (2012). From surviving to thriving during transitions. In L. A. Schreiner, M. C. Louis, & D. D. Nelson (Eds.), *Thriving in transitions: A research-based approach to college student success* (pp. 1-18). Columbia, SC: University of South Carolina, National Resource Center for The First-Year Experience & Students in Transition.

Schreiner, L. A., Kalinkewicz, L., McIntosh, E. J., & Cuevas, A. P. (2013, November). *Advancing a psychosocial model of college student success: The role of thriving.* Paper presented at the annual meeting of the Association for the Study of Higher Education, St. Louis, MO.

Schreiner, L. A., Louis, M. C., & Nelson, D. D. (Eds.). (2012). *Thriving in transitions: A research-based approach to college student success.* Columbia, SC: University of South Carolina, National Resource Center for The First Year Experience & Students in Transitions.

Schreiner, L. A., Nelson, D. D., & Louis, M.C. (2012). Recommendations for facilitating thriving in transitions. In L. A. Schreiner, M. C. Louis, & D. D. Nelson (Eds.), *Thriving in transitions: A research-based approach to college student success* (pp. 191-198). Columbia, SC: University of South Carolina, National Resource Center for The First-Year Experience & Students in Transition.

Tinto, V. (1975). Dropout from higher education: A theoretical synthesis of recent research. *Review of Educational Research, 45,* 89-125.

Tobolowsky, B. F. (2008). Sophomores in transition: The forgotten year. In B. O. Barefoot (Ed.), *The first year and beyond: Rethinking the challenge of collegiate transition* (New Directions for Higher Education No. 144, pp 59-67). San Francisco, CA: Jossey-Bass.

Tobolowsky, B. F., & Cox. B. E. (2007). Findings from the 2005 National Survey on Sophomore Initiatives. In B. F. Tobolowsky & B. E. Cox (Eds.), *Shedding light on sophomores: An exploration of the second college year* (Monograph No. 47, pp. 13-30). Columbia, SC: National Resource Center for The First-Year Experience & Students in Transition.

U.S. Department of Education, National Center for Education Statistics, Integrated Postsecondary Data System. (2013). *Digest of education statistics 2013.* Retrieved from https://nces.ed.gov/programs/coe/pdf/coe_cva.pdf

Wang, M. C., Dziuban, C. D., & Moskal, P. D. (2000). A web-based survey system for distributed learning impact evaluation. *The Internet and Higher Education, 2*(4), 211-220. doi:10.1016/S1096-7516(00)00021-X

About the Authors

Dallin George Young is the assistant director for research, grants, and assessment at the National Resource Center for The First-Year Experience and Students in Transition. He coordinates the research and assessment endeavors of the National Resource Center and facilitates and disseminates three national surveys: the National Survey of First-Year Seminars, the National Survey of Sophomore-Year Initiatives, and the National Survey of Senior Capstone Experiences. He oversees a number of research collaborations and grant opportunities between the National Resource Center and the higher education community and across the University of South Carolina campus. Before joining the Center, Young worked in administrative roles in college student housing and assessment. He has taught sections of University 101, a first-year seminar for students at South Carolina. He holds a bachelor's degree in liberal arts and sciences from Utah State University, a master's degree in higher education and student affairs from Virginia Tech, and a doctorate in college student affairs administration from the University of Georgia. Young's research interests have led to publications and presentations on learning outcomes of postsecondary professional preparation, peer leadership, the impact of professional standards in higher education, and assessment.

Laurie A. Schreiner is professor and chair of the doctoral programs in higher education at Azusa Pacific University. She has taught for more than 30 years, after receiving her PhD in community psychology from the University of Tennessee. She is co-author of the Student Satisfaction Inventory and has co-authored such books as *StrengthsQuest: Discover and Develop Your Strengths in College and Beyond* (2006), *Helping Sophomores Succeed* (2010), and *Thriving in Transitions: A Research-Based Approach to College Student Success* (2012), along with numerous journal articles, including a three-part series on college student thriving for *About Campus* (2010). Schreiner is co-editor of the peer-reviewed research journal *Christian Higher Education: An International Journal of Research, Theory, and Practice* and has served on the advisory board of the National Resource Center for The First-Year Experience and Students in Transition and the editorial board for the *Journal of The First-Year Experience & Students in Transition*. Author of the *Thriving Quotient*, Schreiner maintains an active research program on college student thriving.

Eric James McIntosh has worked in student affairs for the past 12 years and is now as a strategic partnerships advisor for Civitas Learning, a higher education technology firm located in Austin, Texas. Using a cloud-based, predictive analytics platform and engaging applications, Civitas Learning helps partner institutions bring deep insights to decision makers and personalized, real-time recommendations directly to the front lines for students, faculty, and advisors to measurably improve student learning, persistence, and graduation. McIntosh completed his PhD at Azusa Pacific University in higher education with a dissertation entitled *Thriving in College: The Role of Spirituality and Psychological Sense of Community in Students of Color*. A member of the research team at the Thriving Project, his research interests include student success, spirituality, retention, and access for underrepresented student populations.